Ffoshelig Coaches Ltd
Carmarthen

Published by Vernon Morgan

September 2021

ISBN: 978-0-9574045-7-1

© Copyright Vernon Morgan (2021)

All photographs are from the author's collection, unless otherwise stated.

All rights reserved. No part of this book may be reproduced or transmitted in any form, or by any means, electronic or mechanical, including photocopying, recording or by any information storage and retrieval system without permission from the publisher in writing.

Other titles published by the same author:

James of Ammanford.	(A history of J. James & Sons Ltd, Ammanford, and Jones Bros [Brynteg] Up Tumble).
SWT 100.	(The South Wales Transport Co. Ltd, centenary).
Images of Old Llanelli & District.	(Historical views of Llanelli & District).
Saml. Eynon & Sons 'The Hero', Trimsaran.	(A history of Samuel Eynon & Sons).
Silcox Motor Coach Co Ltd, Pembroke Dock.	(A history of Silcox Motor Coach Co Ltd).
Davies Bros (Pencader) Ltd.	(A history of Davies Bros [Pencader] Ltd).
Rees & Williams Ltd, and West Wales Motors Ltd. Tycroes, Ammanford. 'The Friendly Rivals'.	(A history of both companies, together with Peter Smith/Triafon Motors Ltd, Garnswllt).

Cover Picture: This integrally built Optare 'Versa' V1100, with B38F layout, **YJ59 NMZ** was purchased initially for the 222, Carmarthen to Pendine service, and arrived in November 2009. It was captured here on 11th February 2010, leaving Carmarthen bus station for its final destination, Carmarthen Railway Station, situated a hundred metres from the bus station, but ¼ mile by road, along Coracle Way, over the river Towy bridge, and Station Approach. *(V. Morgan).*

Rear Cover: **VFH 700S** was an immaculate Leyland 'Leopard' PSU3C/4R acquired by the intermediate proprietor of Ffoshelig Coaches, Des Jones, in May 1983, to replace a Bedford YMT. Des Jones was a son of David Jones the founder of Ffoshelig. This grant specification vehicle was one of the last few Mk I Duple 'Dominant' bodies built on a 'Leopard' chassis in September 1977, for Pullham, Bourton-on-the-Water, Gloucestershire. *(Jason Feeley collection).*

Title Page: Pictured here is the current proprietor and managing director of Ffoshelig Coaches Ltd, Phillip Rhodri Evans, after taking delivery of his first brand new vehicle in September 1999, a Berkhof 'Axial 50' bodied Dennis Javelin, registered with cherished registration, **V2 FOS**. *(Courtesy of Rhodri Evans).*

AUTHORS ACKNOWLEDGEMENTS

It's been an enormous challenge to produce this publication in time for the company's centenary, due to the fact that my previous title was only published eleven months earlier, in October 2020, coupled with the national lockdown, brought about by the Coronavirus pandemic, and the closing of public libraries and archives.

In addition to all that, I am a full time Carer for my wife, who has Alzheimer's dementia.

Nevertheless, as always, I have enjoyed compiling this publication, and I am indebted to numerous people for their sincere help and assistance in compiling it.

First of all, I would like to single out and thank Rhodri Evans, the current Managing Director of Ffoshelig Coaches, for his enthusiastic help and assistance. Rhodri has given up his precious time talking to me, and answering hundreds of questions by countless e-mails and phone calls, during the Coronavirus pandemic, and at the same time, very kindly provided numerous excellent photographs and memorabilia for inclusion in this publication.

My sincere thanks are also tendered to Rhydian Jones, grandson of David Jones, the founder of Ffoshelig Coaches. Rhydian made available the family's collection of early photographs, and provided a wealth of information regarding the company's early beginnings.

Thanks also to the voluntary staff at 'The Bus Archive', Walsall, and the 'CBPG' Archive at Barry, for allowing access to their archive material, and to fellow bus enthusiasts, John Bennett, John Jones, Richard Evans, Michael Taylor, David Donati, John Martin, Roy Marshall, Robert Mack, Alan Cross, Don Jones (LTBPS), R.H.G. Simpson, Peter Yeomans, Eric Wain, and Jason Feeley, for their enthusiastic help and encouragement, providing photographs, memorabilia and information, not forgetting Daniel James for the aerial view of Maes-y-Prior, taken by Drone.

Although, most photographs are views taken by myself, or views from my extensive collection, I must point out that it has not always been possible to identify individual photographers. No discourtesy is intended through lack of acknowledgement, in view of which, I trust they will accept my sincere thanks.

Much other valuable information has come from material in the care of 'The PSV Circle', and Carmarthenshire County Council Cultural Services Department, not forgetting the information contained in the 'Welsh Bus & Coach Newsletter'.

Finally, I would like to tender my grateful thanks to Katie, my daughter, for her contribution towards this publication. Katie proofread my draft, and corrected small grammatical errors.

CONTENTS

AUTHORS ACKNOWLEDGEMENTS	4
CONTENTS	5
INTRODUCTION	6
HOW THE BUSINESS STARTED	7
EFFECTS OF THE ROAD TRAFFIC ACT (1930)	13
TIME FOR CHANGE	31
THE EFFECTS OF DEREGULATION	65
FFOSHELIG COACHES UNDER NEW OWNERSHIP	81
INCORPORATION	131
D. JONES (FFOSHELIG COACHES) VEHICLE DETAILS	155
P.R. EVANS (FFOSHELIG COACHES) VEHICLE DETAILS	161
D. JONES (FFOSHELIG COACHES) VEHICLE DISPOSALS	168
P.R. EVANS (FFOSHELIG COACHES) VEHICLE DISPOSALS	171
VEHICLE PHOTOGRAPH INDEX	175

INTRODUCTION

This publication has been produced to celebrate the centenary of 'Ffoshelig Coaches', currently the longest serving independent passenger vehicle operator in South Wales. Simultaneously, it marks the 25th anniversary of the business's current proprietor.

David Jones, founder of the 'Ffoshelig Coaches' business, was originally a farmer at Ffoshelig Farm, Newchurch, near Carmarthen. He diversified from farming into road transport soon after World War 1 ended, with a haulage business, which shortly afterwards included an omnibus, when he inaugurated a motor-bus service.

He inaugurated the first passenger service to serve the hamlet and parish of Newchurch, and it can truly be said that David Jones was the 'pioneer' of public transport in that extremely rural community of north-west Carmarthenshire. He was quickly followed by numerous competitors, who fell by the wayside, or were eventually absorbed. The haulage business was eventually sold to a local competitor, in order to concentrate entirely on passenger transport.

One of his two sons, David Desmond Jones (known as Des), eventually joined the business after relinquishing his teaching post, taking over the business upon his father's retirement. Des modernised the fleet with new and second-hand coaches, expanded the network of services, and introduced a tours programme, which included Holiday Tours. Furthermore, he built a completely new workshop at the depot.

Des Jones however, decided to retire from the business, on the company's 75th anniversary in 1996, but strangely, no one was prepared to absorb the whole business, resulting in its break up into three parts.

Former part-time 'Ffoshelig' driver, Phillip Rhodri Evans, who similarly had a background in farming, absorbed the main portion of the business.

Rhodri had already established himself as a coach operator some nine months earlier, operating from the family's farm, at St Peters, Carmarthen, and after absorbing the larger portion of Ffoshelig's business, moved his operating centre into Ffoshelig Garage, at Newchurch, maintaining the same high standards as his predecessors, the Jones family, retaining the Ffoshelig Coaches title along with the livery.

As time progressed, the business expanded and retreated back to Rhodri Evans' original premises at Maes-y-Prior, St Peters, Carmarthen, where it remains today, in 2021.

Finally, I would like to wish the directors of Ffoshelig Coaches, Rhodri and Debbie Evans, their continued success, and hopefully another 100 years of 'first class' service.

HOW THE BUSINESS STARTED

The origins of 'Ffoshelig Coaches' can be traced back to 1898, when David Jones was born and brought up at 'Ffoshelig Farm' (originally spelt 'Ffoshelyg'), situated on Blaen-y-coed Road, Newchurch, some 3½ miles north of Carmarthen town.

After the 'Great War' hostilities were over in 1919, he began taking produce from the farm to Carmarthen market, by horse and cart on the town's market days of Wednesday and Saturday, and a year later in May 1920, he purchased his first motor vehicle for that work.

This was a green liveried Vulcan 20hp lorry registered BX 1277, fitted with van type bodywork, and purely by coincidence, one registration number *after* the first motor vehicle of William John Davies, New Inn, (BX 1276), the founder of Davies Brothers, Pencader.

Besides carrying produce to Carmarthen market, the lorry was used to carry livestock to the Carmarthen livestock market, and after carrying out that duty, it would be taken back to the farm, washed out, and equipped with bench seats to carry local passengers, including local farmers' wives with *their* produce to sell in the market.

In addition to the lorry, a motor cycle and side car was acquired in 1921-2, and used as a 'taxi'. The second hand motor cycle, registered DW 293, was fitted with a side car resembling a miniature bus, and is pictured here on the right hand side.

The successful market day service, which was inaugurated in 1921, was an offshoot to the haulage business already set up by David Jones. The service, which was unlicensed, started from Pantywaun, two miles north of Blaen-y-coed, in rural north-west Carmarthenshire, and ran via Blaen-y-coed, Bwlchnewydd, Henfwlch, and Trevaughan into Carmarthen. The service became so popular, it quickly warranted a bus on the route.

The service was 'unlicensed' due to the fact that Carmarthen Borough Council didn't start licensing passenger services, or public service vehicles until early 1926.

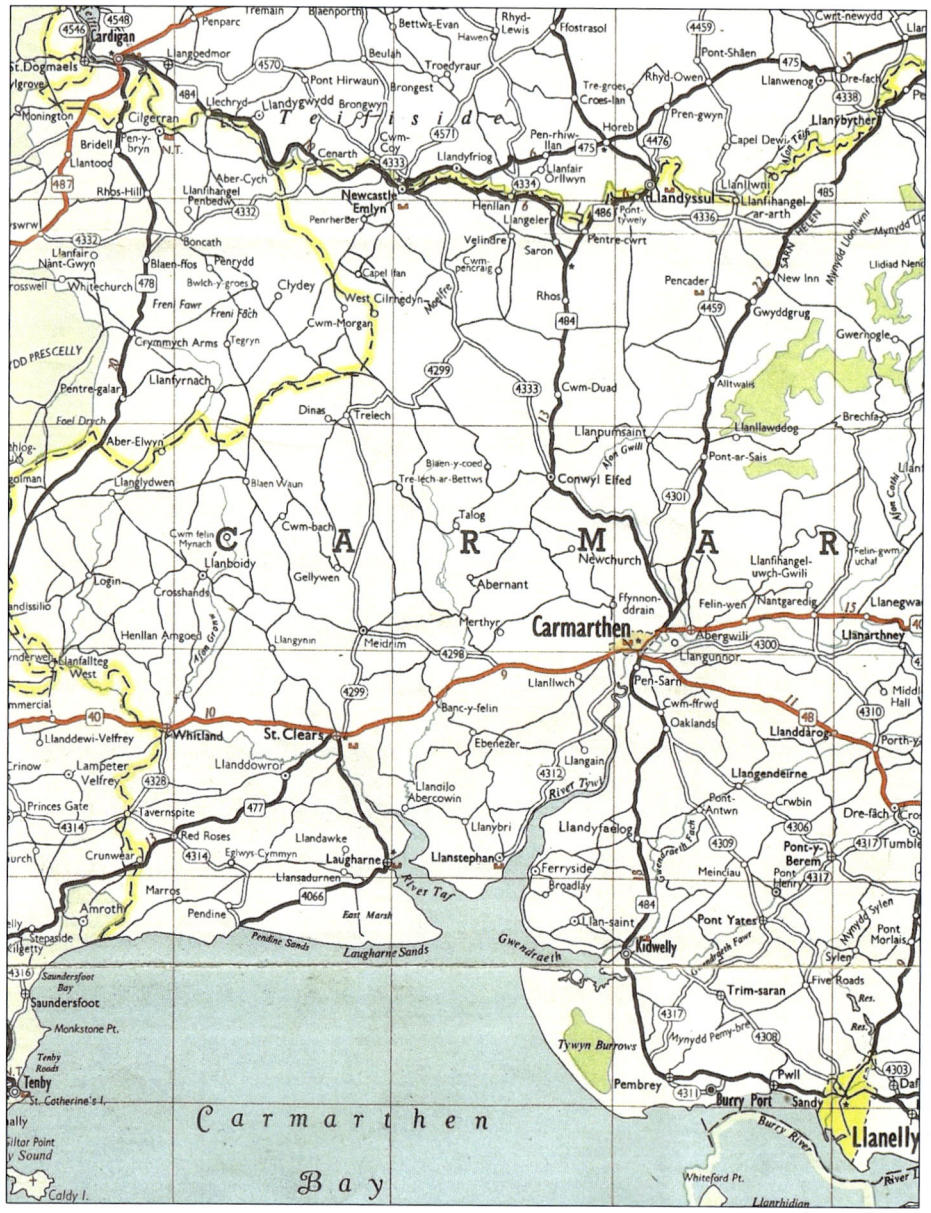

Above: This map of north-west Carmarthenshire, shows the location of Newchurch and the surrounding villages mentioned in the story, all situated on a network of unclassified roads, northward of the A40 trunk road.

Above: 'Newchurch Pride' was a fleet name used by David Jones' on his first omnibus in 1921, a 20 seat Daimler. Precice details of this vehicle can not be found, but is thought to have been acquired second-hand.
(Courtesy of Rhydian Jones - David Jones' grandson).

At that point, David Jones had 'slipped through the net'. He didn't apply for the necessary licences, probably due to the fact that his terminal point at the main entrance of Carmarthen market, in St Catherine Street, was out of sight from the council's licensing inspectors who observed the town's bus services at the main bus termini, in Lammas Street and Guildhall Square.

However, bearing in mind that Newchurch lay in a remote area of rural Carmarthenshire, the neighbourhood had numerous hackney carriage operators in those early days, all named 'Jones', who competed with large motor cars and/or small capacity buses.

Ironically, by March 1924, there was a second David Jones, who operated a hackney licensed vehicle registered BX 4236, from Bryndawel, Trelech. There was a Thomas Jones at Corner House, Newchurch, with a hackney licensed vehicle registered BX 4899 in 1924, and a John Jones at Waterloo House, Trelech, by January 1924, operating BX 4095, and by January 1925, H. James Jones, of Penybont, was running a small charabanc registered BX 5277. A third hackney carriage operator at Trelech was Trevor Davies of Blaenant Fawr, who bought a vehicle registered BX 4534, in May 1924.

Incidentally, Trelech, Talog, Penybont, Abernant, Blaen-y-waun and Bwlchnewydd, are all hamlets of the neighbouring parish, Abernant, and another neighbouring parish Mydrim, (later Meidrim) also had their share of operators, namely David Evans, Henry Daniel Jenkins and John Rees Davies, all situated within the village of Mydrim.

Above: When David Jones bought this 20 seat Guy BA, registered **BX 7410** in December 1926, the fleetname 'Newchurch Express' replaced the name 'Newchurch Pride', due to the fact it was fitted with pneumatic tyres, which under new legislation, was permitted to travel at 20 mph, compared to 12 mph for vehicles fitted with solid tyres. *(Courtesy of Rhydian Jones).*

In May 1927, Carmarthen Borough Council licensing committee granted Thomas Jones of Abernant, a licence for a service between Abernant and Carmarthen via Blaenwaun. This is believed to be the same Thomas Jones, who previously operated from Corner House, Newchurch. At the same licensing committee meeting, David Jones, Ffoshelig was issued with his first road service licence for the Pantywaun – Blaen-y-coed – Bwlchnewydd – Carmarthen service, and two years later in April 1929, he received an extra hackney carriage licence for a second vehicle.

However, when Carmarthen Borough Council issued their annual road service licences in April 1930, competitor Thomas Jones was granted Blaenwaun to Carmarthen, which partly ran on David Jones's route, and David Jones was granted Capel Cendy (near Abernant) to Carmarthen, a licence not renewed upon introduction of the Traffic Act in April 1931.

Above: This is another view of David Jones' Guy BA, 20 seater, **BX 7410**, which came to grief near Aberaeron, whilst taking a group of gentlemen, possibly farmers, on an outing to Aberystwyth. The roof mounted luggage rack would have been used regularly on the market day service, carrying farm produce into Carmarthen market. *(Courtesy of Rhydian Jones).*

Above: This partial view of the Guy BA, **BX 7410** has been included specifically as a tribute to David Jones, the founder of Ffoshelig Coaches. He is the gentleman standing on the right-hand side of the view. *(Courtesy of Rhydian Jones).*

Above: Another view of the Guy BA, **BX 7410**, which is seen on the previous page, shows a detatchable luggage carrier fitted to the front of the bus. This was used to carry farm produce to Carmarthen market on market days, besides the luggage rack fitted to its roof, which is clearly seen in the view on the previous page. This vehicle had been sold to Gimblett Motors, Llanelly, by 1932, where it apears to have ended its days. *(Courtesy of Rhydian Jones).*

At the same time, David Jones found he had another competitor on the Carmarthen route, when John Rees Davies of Mydrim (later Talog), started running a service from Trelech to Carmarthen via Penybont, Talog, Bwlchnewydd, Henfwlch and Trevaughan.

Competition between all these operators, in such a sparsely populated area, became quite a challenge, and could be described as 'the survival of the fittest'.

Nevertheless, in October 1930, David Jones purchased a new Morris Commercial tipper lorry for the haulage business, and supporting local tradespeople, purchased it from the Morris dealership of 'Lowndes Motors', at Priory Street, Carmarthen. This was registered TH 1209, and was followed in February 1932, by a second Morris Commercial tipper registered TH 2283.

EFFECTS OF THE ROAD TRAFFIC ACT (1930)

The next major event in the company's history was The Road Traffic Act (1930), which became a 'godsend' to most operators, but was not the case for David Jones.

This Act of Parliament, which was passed in August 1930, gave the Ministry of Transport's Traffic Commissioners full control of public service vehicles (PSVs), together with passenger services and their licensing in Great Britain.

These Traffic Commissioners, with the power vested in them, brought about improved operating conditions, adherence to timetables, and stability of fares. All stage carriage and express service routes had to be licensed, and the granting of such licences, which had previously been under the jurisdiction of the local authorities, were then only obtainable through the Ministry of Transport's Traffic Commissioners. Licences to drive and conduct a PSV, also became the Traffic Commissioners responsibility. Under this new licensing system, all PSV operators were issued with operator reference numbers, by which they were identified. Consequently, the number issued to David Jones, was TGR 364, with each road service licence applied for thereafter being given licence application numbers beginning with the operator reference number.

After implementing the new Traffic Act fully in April 1931, every bus and coach operator had to re-apply to the new authority for renewal of each licence held, and re-apply annually thereafter. Likewise, any changes to services, times, fares or new routes all had to be applied for, and the licences would only be granted when approved by the Traffic Commissioners. However, the only licence that David Jones applied for under the new Traffic Act in April 1931, was a licence to continue running the following stage carriage service:-

TGR 364/1   **Pantywaun** to **Carmarthen (St Catherine Street)**.
via Blaen-y-coed, Bwlchnewydd and Trevaughan.
Service to operate on Mondays, Wednesdays, Saturdays and fair days only.
Granted on 29th September 1931.
Modification to start from **Maniwan**, granted 4/10/1932.
Modification to discontinue the Monday service, granted 3/10/1933.

The following licence was applied for on 3rd June, 1931:-

TGR 365/2   **Excursions & Tours** starting from Pantywaun, Blaen-y-coed and district.
[1] Newcastle Emlyn fair.
[2] Carmarthen fair.
[3] St Clears fair.
[4] Other Excursions & Tours on special occasions.
All tours to run throughout the year.
Granted on 29th September, 1931, with an amendment: all Excursions & Tours to start from <u>Newchurch</u>.

Above: This view, taken outside the 'Spring Well' public house, Pendine, depicts **TX 8740**, a 1930, 20 seat GMC T30, acquired from Osborne Bus Services, Neath in April 1931, and **TH 2510**, a Bedford WHB, with Duple C14F bodywork, which David Jones acquired new in May 1932, the only two passenger vehicles owned between 1932 & 1937. *(Courtesy of Rhydian Jones).*

Introduction of the aforementioned Road Traffic Act, was certainly no help to David Jones. Within five months of the Ministry of Transport taking control, competition against him was allowed to increase.

Two rival operators were granted additional licences in September 1931, to operate individual services from Trelech to Carmarthen, which travelled predominantly on David Jones' route, without restrictions.

John Rees Davies of Mydrim was granted a second route from Trelech to Carmarthen, albeit on a slightly different route, via Blaen-y-coed, Bwlchnewydd, Henfwlch Road, and Trevaughan on a *daily* basis, and Henry Daniel Jenkins of Mydrim was granted Trelech to Carmarthen via Post Gwyn, Blaen-y-coed, Bwlchnewydd, Henfwlch Road and Trevaughan, to run on market days only (Wednesdays/Saturdays), the same days as David Jones.

Davies' daily service into Carmarthen was not viable, and coupled with the loss of a bus destroyed by fire on 28th March, 1932, he withdrew this service in September 1932.

And in August 1933, H.D. Jenkins applied for John Rees Davies' Trelech – Penybont – Bwlchnewydd – Carmarthen, road service licence. He was immediately issued with five temporary licences to operate the service until 6th October, 1933, but the transfer was eventually refused. Davies then continued operating this service himself, but moved from Mydrim to live at the nearby village of Talog, in July 1934.

Incidentally, John Rees Davies' business eventually passed to David Jones, Ffoshelig in 1947.

Returning to October 1931, another ambitious 'Jones', Daniel Emrys Jones, of Towerhill Stores, Trelech, decided to apply for a road service licence, to run a competitive service of stage carriage from Trelech to Carmarthen, via Maniwan, Pantywaun, and Blaen-y-coed village, operating one return journey on Saturdays only, with a 14 seat bus registered BX 8474.

After objections from the established licence holders in the community, D.E. Jones withdrew his application, and disappeared without further trace.

Despite all those operational difficulties, David Jones battled on, and applied for a 'new' stage carriage service licence on 8th June, 1932:-

TGR 364/3 **Carmarthen (St Catherine Street)** to **Carmarthen Golf Links (Blaen-y-coed Road)**, via Ffynnonddrain.
To operate Monday – Saturday, all year round. Fare 6d return.
Granted 4/10/1932.

Above: Two other operators from north-west Carmarthenshire with registered market day services into Carmarthen, were Henry Edward Clarke of Capel Evan (Capel Iwan), Newcastle Emlyn, trading as Clarke Bros., with **TH 1068**, a 14 seat Chevrolet, locally bodied by Thomas & Thomas, of Carmarthen, and David Edward Williams, Velindre, with his 20 seat Dodge, **TH 1928**, which was probably also bodied by Thomas & Thomas. *(John Martin collection).*

Above and below: This Morris Commercial tipper lorry, **TH 2283**, was new to David Jones, Ffoshelig in February 1932.
(CBPG Archive).

In the meantime, the omnibus sector of David Jones' business had a difficult time with all the rivalry going on, and remained tranquil with just two buses during the depression of the 1930s, increasing to three buses in 1937. His business at this particular point in time was mainly haulage. He held five 'A' licences, and was operating five lorries.

The Lorries were engaged on daily milk collections (in milk churns), from farms throughout the area, for the Creameries at Carmarthen and Whitland, besides carrying white lime, to farms around the county. White lime is used by farmers to raise the pH (potential of hydrogen) levels in soil.

World War 2 years, however, were equally as quiet for the passenger business, except for the issue of three licences, TGR 364/4-6, and the absorption of one road service licence from H.D. Jenkins in 1944, under defence permit, which was incorporated into David Jones' TGR 364/1 road service licence, upon instruction of the Ministry of War Transport, (see below).

However, all licence applications during WW2 had to be authorised by the Ministry of War Transport, and the additional licences issued to David Jones, subsequent to September 1939, are listed below:-

TGR 364/4   Was a licence issued to operate a workers express carriage service to **Trecwn (RNAD)**
Precise details are unavailable.

TGR 364/5   **Abernant** to **Carmarthen (St. Catherine Street)**.
via: Merthyr, Henfwlch and Trevaughan. (Wednesdays only).

TGR 364/6   **Conwil Elfed** to **Carmarthen**.
via: Penrhiwcynfryn, Bwlchnewydd, Trawsmawr, Henfwlch Road, and Trevaughan. (Monday – Saturday).

And in 1944, a modification was carried out to the following road service licence:

TGR 364/1   Route extended to commence from **Postgwyn**, when H.D. Jenkins of Talog withdrew his Wednesdays/Saturdays only, Trelech, Postgwyn, Blaen-y-coed, Carmarthen service, which ran parallel to David Jones' service. *(Suspected to be on direction of the Ministry of War Transport, to save on wasteful duplication).*

Authorisation of the above Conwil Elfed to Carmarthen service, TGR 364/6, required an extra vehicle in the fleet, which consequently led to the authorisation and purchase of a Bedford OWB, registered BTH 777, in October 1942. Fourteen months later, in December 1943, another new Bedford was authorised by the Ministry of War Transport, a Bedford lorry (CBX 160) for the haulage business.

Above: The cover of a brochure for the Bedford OWB utility bus. Its cost, finished in semi-gloss brown primer, was £810.

Above: Pictured here on lay-over at Lammas Street, Carmarthen, in 1950, is **BTH 777**, a Duple utility bodied Bedford OWB, which was new to David Jones in October 1942. It was the only vehicle acquired during World War 2. *(Alan B Cross).*

After the wartime hostilities were over, the Ministry of Transport's Traffic Commissioners regained control of all aspects of PSV licensing from the Ministry of War Transport. At that point, David Jones applied for annual renewal of his licences, which were all granted in December 1946. A few months later, the Conwil Elfed - Carmarthen licence, TGR 364/6, which had previously operated on a 'Defence Permit', was revoked after objections from Western Welsh O.C., as to its starting point at Conwil Elfed. The licence was re-applied for on 12th November, 1947, and eventually reinstated in April 1948, with a modification which shortened the route by one mile, to start from Penrhiwcynfryn, running its normal route via Bwlchnewydd, Trawsmawr, Henfwlch, and Trevaughan, Mondays to Saturdays.

It must be noted that David Jones had a penchant for triple digit registration marks, and in October 1946, a Bedford OYD lorry arrived for the haulage business, registered CTH 555.

On the other hand, the omnibus side of the business only moderately expanded, and in December 1946, negotiations took place with rival operator John Rees Davies of Talog, in view of absorbing his business. Consequently, Davies' only two licences were applied for:-

TGR 364/7   **Trelech** to **Carmarthen**
                via: Penybont, Talog, Bwlchnewydd, Henfwlch, and Trevaughan.
                Daily, Mondays to Saturdays.
                Previously licensed to John Rees Davies on TGR 283/1.

TGR 364/8   **Excursions & Tours** starting from Trelech.   (Applied for on 22/1/1947).
Previously licensed to John Rees Davies, Talog, on TGR 283/2.

Both licences were granted in March 1947, and the business was acquired together with an elderly Ford 'BB', 20 seat bus, registered TH 4455, dating from 1934. Incidentally, Ford commercial vehicles of the day were badged as 'Fordson'. This ageing bus with its 4 cylinder petrol engine, rated at 24hp, was not retained. It was soon replaced by a 1939, Duple bodied Bedford WTB, which is seen below.

<u>Above:</u> This 1939 Bedford WTB with Duple C26F coachwork, **SX 5044**, was a replacement for the Fordson 'BB' 20 seater, which had been acquired with the business of J.R. Davies, Talog, in March 1947. The Bedford WTB resembled the later Bedford OB, which superseded the WTB in 1939, having more-or-less the same mechanical components, a 6 cylinder, 28hp petrol engine, 4 speed sliding mesh gearbox and servo assisted hydraulic brakes.   *(Courtesy of Rhydian Jones).*

At the same time in January 1947, David Jones applied for another new licence:-

TGR 364/9   **Excursions & Tours** starting from Conwil Elfed village.

Objections were received once again from the Western Welsh Omnibus Co, and after a public hearing, the licence was refused on 9th July, 1947.

Above: This view of an unknown outing was found with some Ffoshelig paperwork, and is presumed to be a David Jones, Ffoshelig vehicle, but can not be identified. Could it be the Ford 'BB' acquired from J.R. Davies, **TH 4455**? *(CBPG collection).*

Above: Another unidentified view that was found with the Ffoshelig paperwork, is this one taken at Porthcawl. The vehicle is presumed to be **TH 9099**, a 1937 Bedford WTB, with Thomas & Thomas bodywork. *(CBPG collection).*

Above: David Jones' fleet in 1949/50, was predominantly Bedford, as shown here on an outing to Porthcawl in 1949, with drivers, Denzil, Ogwyn, Dai Bach and Iorwerth. Left to right, the vehicles are, **SX 5044** a Bedford WTB, accompanied by Bedford OBs, **DTH 999**, **ETH 888** and **EBX 666**. *(Courtesy of Rhydian Jones).*

Above: Having experienced the Bedford marque for 16 years, David Jones purchased his first Bedford OB, **DTH 999**, fitted with Duple 'Vista' C29F bodywork in April 1948. The ubiquitous OB was ideally suited for the narrow country lanes served by David Jones, and could be found in large numbers operating rural services throughout the country. It can safely be said that the Bedford OB made its presence in most bus fleets, large and small, during the post war years. **DTH 999** is captured here at Lammas Street, Carmarthen, in 1958, preparing to depart for Bwlchnewydd. *(Roy Marshall).*

Nevertheless, eager to expand his network of services further, David Jones applied to the Traffic Commissioners for another 'new' road service licence on 3rd March, 1948:-

TGR 364/10 **Trelech** to **Carmarthen**
via: Groesffordd, Pantygroes, Mydrim, Sarnbwla and Llethrach.
To run on Wednesdays and Saturdays only.

This particular 'stage carriage' licence, had previously been issued to rival, Henry Daniel Jenkins of Mydrim, and became available due to Jenkins' retirement. Jenkins' other Wednesday and Saturday market day service from Mydrim to Carmarthen, had passed to Tudor Williams & Brothers, Laugharne (t/a Pioneer Buses) during WW2. His Friday only service, Mydrim to Newcastle Emlyn, passed to H.E. Clarke, of Capel Evan.

However, Tudor Williams & Bros. and Western Welsh Omnibus Co. objected to David Jones' above application, which resulted in a public hearing on 23rd July, 1948, at The Crown Court, Shire Hall, Carmarthen, where the licence was granted.

At the same hearing, David Jones objected to Tudor Williams & Bros' application to modify their Wednesday & Saturday Mydrim to Carmarthen service. The Williams brothers were asking for an extension to their service, to start from Trelech instead of Mydrim, but they subsequently withdrew their request.

Left: **EBX 666** was another Bedford OB in the fleet with Duple 'Vista' C29F coachwork, which was acquired new in July 1948. This one was withdrawn after 11 years of continuous service, and was replaced by a second-hand Bedford OB, dating from 1950.
(Courtesy of Rhydian Jones).

On 9th November, 1949, David Jones asked to modify his Wednesdays only Abernant to Carmarthen service (TGR 364/5), to include a Saturday service, as shown on next page. The starting point of Trallwn, actually Trallwyn, is a large house in the village of Abernant.

364/5—**David Jones,** of Ffoshelig, Newchurch, Carmarthen. Stage carriages between Abernant and Carmarthen. Revised time table :—

		WO	SO
	a.m.	a.m.	a.m.
Trallwn .. .. .. dep.	8 15	9 30	10 5
Capel Cendy .. .. .. ,,	8 20	9 35	10 15
Ricketts Mill .. .. .. ,,	8 30	9 45	10 20
Merthyr (Cross Roads) .. dep.	8 35	9 50	10 25
Tynewydd (Cross Roads) .. ,,	8 40	9 55	10 30
Henfwlch .. .. .. ,,	8 45	10 0	10 40
Trevaughan .. .. .. ,,	8 55	10 10	10 45
Carmarthen .. .. .. arr.	9 0	10 15	—
			WS
	p.m.	p.m.	p.m.
Carmarthen .. .. .. dep.	4 15	—	3 30
Trevaughan .. .. .. ,,	4 20	—	3 35
Henfwlch .. .. .. ,,	4 30	—	3 45
Tynewydd (Cross Roads) .. ,,	4 35	—	3 50
Merthyr (Cross Roads) .. ,,	4 40	—	3 55
Ricketts Mill .. .. .. ,,	4 50	—	4 5
Capel Cendy .. .. .. ,,	4 55	—	4 10
Trallwn .. .. .. arr.	5 0	—	4 15

WO—Wednesdays only. SO—Saturdays only.
WS—Wednesdays and Saturdays.

The above modifications were granted on 8th December, 1949, but a short time later reverted to Wednesdays only, and was eventually discontinued on 12th April, 1961, when it changed to one morning inward journey, and one afternoon outward journey, on schooldays only.

Above: It would have been a familier sight in the 1950s to find one of Jones Ffoshelig's Bedfords on lay-over here at Brickyard Lane, adjacent to Carmarthen Park and also at St Davids Avenue, Carmarthen. They would have been awaiting departure time for their once weekly destinations of Mydrim, Abernant, and Trelech. This Bedford OB, **ETH 888**, with Mulliner B31F bodywork, was new to Jones in April 1949. *(Don Jones, LTBPS).*

Above: New to Richards Bros, Moylegrove, Pembs, in 1943, but acquired from Thomas & Jones (Precelly Motors) Efail Wen, Pembs, in August 1951, is David Jones' rather battle scarred Bedford OWB, **FDE 623**, with Duple utility bodywork. It is pictured outside the Drovers Arms, Lammas Street, Carmarthen, loading up for a return journey to Bwlchnewydd in the mid -1950s. Also visible in this view are the Harp Inn, John Bowen the Ironmongers, Edwards Cycles and the County Stores. *(LTBPS)*.

Above: In December 1955, this former Eastern National, Bedford OB, **LPU 620**, with Beadle B30F bodywork was acquired from D.J. Morrison, Tenby. It is seen here working a private outing to the seaside village of Llanstephan. *(R.H.G. Simpson)*.

Above: Another shot of the Beadle bodied Bedford OB, **LPU 620**, this time between duties, at St. Davids Avenue, Carmarthen. It's acompanied by David Jones' Duple 'Vista' bodied Bedford OB, **EBX 666**, in July 1959. *(V. Morgan collection).*

Above: In early 1957, David Jones bought two more Beadle B30F bodied Bedford OBs **DBD 936/940** from the well renown fleet of D.J. Morrison, Tenby (28/27). The pair had originally operated in the large fleet of United Counties Omnibus Co. as (119/123). **DBD 936**, seen here at an unknown location, was new in January 1948, and entered service with Jones in March 1957, retaining the dark green wings and window surrounds of Morrison's green & cream livery. Jones' normal livery at this point in time was red with cream relief. *(V. Morgan collection).*

Above: Seen here on lay-over at St. Davids Avenue, Carmarthen, is **DBD 940**, the third Beadle bodied Bedford OB acquired from D.J. Morrison in 1957, which give excellent service until April 1963. All three retained their perol engines. *(Peter Yeomans)*.

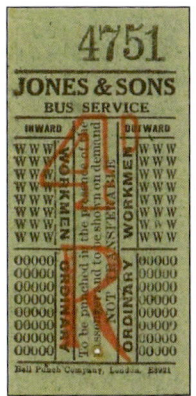
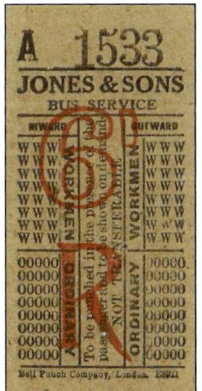
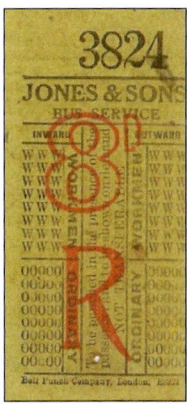

A selection of early David Jones & Sons, 'Bell Punch' bus tickets, with advertisements on the rear for his haulage business.

Above: This Bedford OB, **HCJ 273**, with Duple 'Vista' C29F coachwork arrived in April 1957, from Baynham, Ross-on-Wye, and was the first coach in the fleet to receive the company's new livery of cream and pale blue. This view was taken on the Lammas Street bus stand, Carmarthen, outside N & A. Lloyd's newsagent shop and E. Evans' ladies fashions. *(R. Marshall).*

Above: Viewed at the same location in Carmarthen, loading up for Abernant, is **HSG 231**, another Duple 'Vista' bodied Bedford OB, which came from a Scottish operator in 1959. It was the second vehicle to receive the new company livery. *(Roy Marshall).*

Above: A late 1950s aerial view of David Jones & Sons' depot, 'Ffoshelig Garage', show two Duple 'Vista' bodied Bedford OBs inside the *nearest* barn type garage, with a Beadle bodied example in the second garage. *(Courtesy of Rhydian Jones).*

Above: This 1957 view of Lammas St, Carmarthen, shows DTH 999, on the same stand as HSG 231, pictured opposite.

Above: David Jones & Sons acquired this 1948 Duple 'Vista' bodied Bedford OB, **LUA 541** from D.S. Davies (Red & Green Coaches) of New Inn, Pencader, in December 1962. It retained the 'Red & Green' livery throughout its 3 year operational period at David Jones, and was taken out of service in December 1965, to be cannibalised for spare parts.   *(V. Morgan collection).*

TIME FOR CHANGE

As we have seen earlier, a new coach livery of cream and pale blue was introduced in 1957, and to enhance the company image, the fleet-name of 'Ffoshelig Coaches' was introduced soon afterwards. This title was undeniably derived from the garage name, 'Ffoshelig Garage', and David Jones' house opposite the garage, 'Ffoshelig Villa', not forgetting the company's origins at 'Ffoshelig Farm'.

Above: The arrival of this 1955 'butterfly fronted' Bedford SBG, **ASB 658**, with Duple 'Vega' C38F coachwork in April 1963, not only modernised the fleet, but marked the beginning of a new era, with the new fleet-name 'Ffoshelig Coaches'. This view was taken outside the now extinct, 'Ystrad Tywi Secondary School,' at Johnstown, Carmarthen, circa 1968. *(R.F. Mack).*

By this point in time, the haulage business had been sold to haulier H. Dewi Evans of Carmarthen, who consequently licensed his lorries as 'H. Dewi Evans (t/a: D. Jones & Sons)'. Selling the haulage concern, slimmed down David Jones' business somewhat, in order to concentrate solely on passenger vehicles, as David Jones' two sons, Desmond and Donald, had decided upon career's elsewhere.

Donald took up an assignment at the famous 'Harrods' store, in Knightsbridge, London, but later joined the 2nd Battalion Parachute Regiment, where he served for 28 years at Northern Ireland and The Falklands, and eventually retired in Northern Ireland. Desmond on the other hand, studied Economics at Liverpool University, and became lightweight boxing champion of the northern universities. Upon leaving university, he took up a teaching assignment at Crymych Grammar School, which became 'Ysgol Y Preseli', Crymych, before returning to Ffoshelig sixteen years later, to take over the business upon his father's retirement.

Nevertheless, a reduction of stage carriage services was inevitable in July 1963, when the Wednesdays only service between Post Gwyn and Carmarthen, became unremunerative. The service was offered to David Thomas Jones (no relation), of Sunnybridge Garage, Abercych, who had originally commenced operating his small PSV business from Trelech, moving to larger premises at the village of Abercych in 1961.

D.T. Jones, made the necessary application for that Carmarthen service on 31st July, 1963, with a modification to start from Abercych, running via Bwlchygroes, Tegryn, Bethel, Blaen-y-coed, Bwlchnewydd, and Trevaughan (23 miles), one journey in each direction, Wednesdays only. He was issued a licence for unforseen service, TGR 4989/Sp/1, to run the service from 11/9/63, to 19/10/63, and the full term licence, TGR 4989/1 was issued on 9th October, 1963. The service was unsuccessful and withdrawn in December 1964, shortly before the intoduction of rural bus service 'Fuel Duty Rebate' in 1965 (see page 36).

With regards to D.T. Jones' garage at Abercych, it had the postal address of Pembrokeshire, but was situated on the eastern side of the village, in Carmarthenshire. (See map on page 8).

Abercych, is a quaint north-east Pembrokeshire village, located at the 'tri-point' of the counties Pembrokeshire, Carmarthenshire and Ceredigion (previously Cardiganshire). The name Abercych (meaning 'Mouth of the Cych') was derived from the name of a river 'Afon Cych', which divides the village as it flows through, marking the boundary between Pembrokeshire and Carmarthenshire. The 'Mouth of the Cych', is at a point just north of the village, where it flows into the river 'Teifi', the 'Teifi' marking the Ceredigion boundary.

Above: Loading up at St Catherine Street, Carmarthen, for the Wednesdays only service mentioned above to Abercych, is **OKH 507**, a Bedford SBG, with Plaxton 'Venturer II' coachwork, owned by D.T. Jones of Abercych.   *(V. Morgan collection)*.

Above: This petrol engine Bedford SBG, **JRN 500**, with superb Plaxton 'Venturer III' C41F coachwork, was purchased by David Jones in May 1964, from Reliance Motors of Cardiff. It's pictured here on Aberavon promenade, working a private charter to that seaside resort, when it was a very popular venue. It's seen here leaving the large car park visible in the backdrop, which also housed the visiting buses and coaches. *(V. Morgan collection).*

Above: Pictured here at Trelech, is **JDK 216**, a very early Bedford SB, with Duple 'Vega' C33F bodywork, which David Jones bought in February 1965, from J. Courtis, of Cardiff. *(V. Morgan collection).*

Above: Captured between school duties in June 1966, at Llanstephan Road, Carmarthen, is this 1948, Mulliner bodied Bedford OB, **EUJ 855**, which was acquired from Roberts, Wellington, Salop, in April 1965. *(V. Morgan collection).*

Above: The first diesel engined vehicle purchased by David Jones was this 'butterfly fronted', Bedford SB3, **BEX 350**, which had been retrofitted with a SB1 diesel engine. Fitted with Duple 'Vega' C41F bodywork, it arrived in October 1966, and remained operational until October 1974. This was new in 1958, to Norfolk M.S. Gt Yarmouth. *(V. Morgan collection).*

Above: With ever increasing fuel costs, economy became of paramount importance, and David Jones soon purchased three more diesel engine vehicles. This 1953 Burlingham 'Seagull' bodied Bedford SB, **HB 7518**, had been retrofitted with a diesel engine by its previous owners, Morlais Motor Services, Merthyr Tydfil, and arrived in December 1966. *(V. Morgan collection).*

Above: A second Burlingham 'Seagull' bodied Bedford SB, **HB 7491**, arrived from Morlais M.S. in January 1967. This one had been retrofitted with a Meadows 4DC diesel engine, and was hardly recognisable after a front end rebuild. It is pictured at Lammas Street, Carmarthen, after making its normal revese manouver into Mansel Street. *(V. Morgan collection).*

Above: **JUO 608** marked the end of an era at 'Ffoshelig' – it was the last normal control vehicle purchased and operated, besides being the last Bedford OB, and the last vehicle with a petrol engine. I have fond memories of this former Devon General (Grey Cars) coach. As a teenager, we used to hire this coach on Saturday evenings from our village operator, E.W. Bonnell, Pwll, for outings to the Coney Beach Firework Display and Amusement Park, Porthcawl. David Jones bought this immaculately kept Duple 'Vega' bodied coach in February 1968, from Gwyn Williams & Sons, Lower Tumble, retaining Williams' livery and fleet number. Sold for preservation in 1971, it is still listed with DVLA, but whereabouts and status are unknown. *(R.F. Mack).*

January 1968, saw the Transport Minister announce details of the Road Traffic Act 1968, which gave stage carriage bus operators financial grants of 25% towards the purchase of new 'service buses', provided they complied with certain requirements of the Ministry of Transport. The intention of the grant scheme was to encourage operators to modernise their fleets and to make buses more competitive with private cars, and in 1970, when the grant was increased to 50%, the rules were extended to include coaches, provided that they were used to a sufficient extent on such bus services, and their coach bodies were built with essential modifications which complied to the bus grant specification. The conditions stipulated that operators would have to refund the grant if they sold the vehicle or ceased to use it for stage carriage service within five years of its delivery.

The scheme commenced on 1st September, 1968, and ended in March 1984, but David Jones did not take up the offer until April 1972, with the purchase of a Bedford YRQ coach. In addition to the bus grant, provision was made to increase the fuel duty rebate introduced in 1965 from 50% to 100%, (10d to 1/7d a gallon), paid to operators of rural bus services from 1st January 1969, together with 'Rural Bus Grants' to subsidise uneconomical rural services.

Above: 125 WRR, was a Bedford SB13 (Leyland 370 cu inch diesel engine), with Duple 'Bella Vega' C41F coachwork, acquired new by Lindrick Coaches, Langold, Nottinghamshire, in June 1964. It was acquired from Lindrick Coaches, in November 1968, and passed to Owens, Knighton, Powys, in 1975. *(V. Morgan collection).*

Above: Another vehicle that never received fleet livery at Ffoshelig was **OKJ 958**, a 1951 Bedford SB, with Duple 'Vega' C33F coachwork, acquired locally from Williams Bros. Upper Tumble, near Llanelli, in 1969. *(V. Morgan collection).*

Above: David Jones & Sons were the third owner of this 1959 Bedford SB8, **TTH 57**, with Duple Midland, B40F bodywork, acquired from Daniel Jones & Sons, Carmarthen. Confusion often arose between these two Jones'. *(Rhydian Jones collection).*

Above: The company's first heavyweight vehicle was **MUH 140**, this former Western Welsh (1140), Leyland 'Tiger Cub' PSUC1/1 with Weymann 'Hermes' B44F bodywork, a breakthrough from the traditional 'Bedford'. It was purchased directly off Western Welsh O.C., complete with WWOC destination blind when they closed their Carmarthen depot in 1971. It served the company until late 1976, when it was replaced by a former Davies Bros, (Pencader) Ltd, Leyland 'Tiger Cub', NBX 581. This view of **MUH 140** was taken at the top end of Blue Street, Carmarthen, near Dark Gate, in 1975. *(R.F. Mack).*

As mentioned on page 36, the government made provisions in the Road Traffic Act (1968), for 'Rural Bus Grants' to subsidise uneconomical rural services. However, at a Carmarthenshire County Council meeting in December 1970, councillors discussed that particular issue, and stated that services should not be subsidised from the rates, they should be subsidised with funding from central government, and refused to allow funding to the Western Welsh O.C. when they applied for subsidies on numerous uneconomical services.

Consequently, Western Welsh gave the mandatory notice to the Traffic Commissioners, and abandoned all of their services operating in West Wales. Their Carmarthen depot at St David's Street, closed on 30th April 1971. And in the meantime, the Traffic Commissioners invited applications from interested parties, for the road service licences previously held by Western Welsh, which resulted in a few erroneous entries published in Notices & Proceedings immediately afterwards. To keep the record straight, it stated that a new company, David Jones & Sons (Newchurch) Ltd, had applied on a new application number, TGR 5255, for all six Carmarthen town services. This has proven to be incorrect. The only application submitted, came from one of the partners of the Daniel Jones & Sons, Abergwili Road, Carmarthen business, using his home address at 101 Bronwydd Rd, Carmarthen.

David Jones (Ffoshelig Coaches) did not apply for any Western Welsh road service licences, but bought one of the Western Welsh Leyland 'Tiger Cubs', using his home address of 44 Lime Grove Avenue, Carmarthen. All six Carmarthen 'town service' licences were applied for, and granted to Daniel Jones & Sons Ltd., Carmarthen, to commence from 1st May 1971.

Above: This depot view of Yeates 'Pegasus' bodied Bedford SB1, **6610 PT** has been included basically for the purpose of showing a rear end shot of the Duple 'Vega' bodied Bedford SBG, **YCV 197**, on the right hand side. It shows the style of signwiting used by 'Ffoshelig Coaches' during the 1960s and 1970s.   *(Eric Wain).*

Above: This Bedford SB1, acquired in July 1971, **6610 PT**, had a rare Yeates 'Pegasus' DP44F body, (bus seats/coach shell), and is seen here leaving Lammas Street, Carmarthen, on route to Meidrim (Mydrim) and Trelech. *(V. Morgan collection).*

Above: The first 'Grant Aided' vehicle purchased by David Jones & Sons was this Duple 'Viceroy' Express C45F bodied Bedford YRQ, in April 1972, registered **STH 800K**, which is seen here at Lammas Street, Carmarthen. *(V. Morgan collection).*

Returning to 1971, a modification was subsequently sought for the Abernant to Carmarthen service, TGR 364/5, on 26th May 1971, to operate an additional journey on schooldays only,

40

from Trevaughan to Ystrad Tywi (High School) and Johnstown (Girls Grammar School). Returning immediately after school hours. Single fares only, at 3 pence each.

Bearing in mind that David Jones did not apply for any of the former Western Welsh services abandoned in 1971, he did not hesitate to apply for the Carmarthen to Llanybri service when it became available three years later. His application read:-

TGR 364/11 **Carmarthen (Lammas Street)** to **Llanybri (Ger-y-Marbell)**.
via: Llanstephan.   Monday to Saturday.
Previously operated by Daniel Jones & Sons Ltd., six daily journeys.

TGR 364/Sp/1 Licence for unforeseen service, issued to operate the above service for the period 5/4/1974 to 30/5/1974, continuing until finally granted.

The above licence was granted 4/12/1974, with modification to operate four journeys daily.

It will be noted that when David Jones took delivery of STH 800K pictured opposite, in April 1972, it was finished in pale blue and mid cream, which was the standard livery. All subsequent deliveries and repaints thereafter, carried the blue and cream livery until September 1985, when the brown, yellow, and cream livery of Aston's, Kempsey, Worcestershire, was adopted – albeit in a different style.

Above: David Jones remained faithful to the Bedford marque for 50 years, and was his preference in April 1974, for a second 'Grant Aided' coach, **XTH 700M**, another Bedford YRQ, seen here with Duple 'Dominant' coachwork. This vehicle was regularly driven by David Jones' daughter-in-law, Irene, until sold to a dealer in 1984, for export to Malta, where it became DBY 411. (See photograph on page 169). *(V. Morgan collection).*

Above: **DRH 122C** was a Bedford SB5 with Plaxton 'Embassy IV' C41F coachwork, acquired from Cwmbran Motors in October 1974, and remained in the fleet until March 1982. It was later scrapped. *(John Jones).*

Above: This Bedford SB8, **LUN 528F**, with Duple 'Bella Vega' C41F coachwork, was also acquired in October 1974, and ran in the livery of its previous owner, Hanmer of Wrexham, for some considerable time before receiving fleet livery. *(V. Morgan).*

Above: As stated opposite, the Bedford SB8, **LUN 528F**, operated in the red and cream livery of its previous owners, Hanmer of Wrexham for some time, as seen here at the depot on 1st October 1977, before its repaint from Hanmer's livery. *(V. Morgan).*

Above: In April 1975, this former Trent M.T. (165) Leyland 'Tiger Cub' PSUC1/2, **VCH 165**, with unmistakable Willowbrook DP41F bodywork, was acquired from J.H. Davies & Co, 'Summerdale Coaches', Letterston, Pembs. *(V. Morgan).*

Above: Only one 'bus' bodied vehicle was purchased with assistance from the 'New Bus Grant', and that was dealer registered **HVJ 146N**, a Bedford YRQ, with Duple 'Dominant' B47F body, in June 1975, seen at Carmarthen 8th February, 1982. The 1963 Singer Gazelle in the backdrop was my every day transport, and after covering 300,000 miles, is now in storage. *(V. Morgan).*

Above: This view of Bedford YRQ, **HVJ 146N**, working the Carmarthen – Talog and Penybont service on 3rd June 1989, displays the new company livery, adopted after the purchase of two Volvo's from Aston of Kempsey. *(V. Morgan collection).*

Above: **MBX 381P** was a 'grant aided' Bedford YLQ, with Duple 'Dominant' Express C45F coachwork, delivered in July 1976.
Below: is a rear end view of the same coach taken on 1st October, 1977, showing its 'all welsh' lettering.   *(V. Morgan).*

Above: The company's new livery was applied to **MBX 381P** by August 1989, when I photographed it here at Carmarthen bus station, working the Wednesdays only, local authority tendered service to Foelgastell. *(V. Morgan).*

On 1st April, 1974, Carmarthenshire County Council amalgamated with the neighbouring counties of Pembrokeshire and Cardiganshire, to form a single county named 'DYFED'. It was unsuccessful, and the three authorities were eventually reinstated on 1st April, 1996. During that period, Dyfed C.C. formed a Passenger Transport Unit named 'BWS DYFED', which controlled all aspects of subsidised bus and rail services in the county.

One of the first projects the newly formed Dyfed C.C. embarked upon was to build a much needed bus station at Carmarthen, which opened at Blue Street, on 3rd August, 1975, (rebuilt in 1997/8), centralising all bus services operating in and out of Carmarthen.

Returning to 1974, David Jones decided to retire from the business at the age of 76, and consequently, handed the business over to his son Desmond Jones.

With no previous experience in transport, David Desmond Jones (Des) took a big step, and relinquished his job as a geography teacher at Ysgol Y Preseli, Crymych, to take the reins at Ffoshelig Coaches, initially, under the watchful eye of his father.

In subsequent years, Des made many improvements, built a new workshop, modernised the fleet and expanded the business. Des' son, Rhydian, assisted his father at the garage as a schoolboy, and took up an engineering apprenticeship there after leaving school in 1979. But sadly, David Jones did not have a long retirement. He passed away on 23rd June, 1977, three weeks before his 79th birthday.

Above: Former Davies Bros (Pencader) Ltd, **NBX 581**, a Leyland 'Tiger Cub' PSUC1/2T, with Willowbrook 45 seat bodywork, arrived in October 1976, and after retaining its Davies Bros livery throughout, was sold for further use in 1978. *(V. Morgan).*

Above: **NFR 837** was a rare Yeates 'Europa' C41F bodied Bedford SB3, retro-fitted with a diesel engine, and was acquired locally from T.M. Thomas, Capel Dewi, for spare parts in January 1977. New in 1958 to Blackhurst, Blackpool, the coachwork was built by W.S. Yeates, Coachbuilders, of Loughborough, who were also bus & coach dealers. *(V. Morgan).*

<u>Above:</u> The first Bristol acquired by Jones, Ffoshelig, was **KHN 730D**, a 1966 Bristol MW6G with Eastern Coachworks B45F bodywork. It was new to United Automobile Services, Darlington, as U730, but was acquired in 1977 from Ribble Motor Services (281), and only saw two years' service at Ffoshelig, before it succumbed to the scrap man's torch.   *(V. Morgan collection).*

<u>Above:</u> The one and only tri-axle vehicle owned by Jones, Ffoshelig was this 1968 Bedford VAL70, with Plaxton 'Panorama II', C52F coachwork, registered **ATU 56F**. It was also the first 11 metre vehicle in the fleet, acquired from Coach Services, Thetford, Norfolk, in October 1977, and passed to Simmons, Maesteg, Mid-Glam., in August 1979.   *(V. Morgan collection).*

Above: This 1961 butterfly fronted, Bedford C5Z1, **608 CYS**, with Duple 'Super Vista' C29F coachwork entered the fleet in September 1978, from Parish, Morda, Shropshire, the first 29 seater in the fleet after a break of 9 years. *(V. Morgan collection).*

Above: **WUX 658K** was a Bedford YRQ with Willowbrook B49F bodywork, which was acquired in September 1978, from Brown, Donnington Wood, but left to join its twin sister, WUX 657K, at Richards Bros, Cardigan, in 1983. *(V. Morgan collection).*

Above: Introduction of the new registration suffix 'V' in August 1979, also introduced a new chassis marque to the Ffoshelig fleet. **FFP 200V** was the company's first experience of a Ford chassis, a Ford R1114, with grant specification Duple 'Dominant II' Express C53F coachwork. This was sold to Mid-Way Motors, Crymych, Pembrokeshire, in August 1994. *(V. Morgan).*

Rationalisation was the order of the day when the road service licence for the daily stage carriage service, Penrhiwcynfryn to Carmarthen, TGR 364/6, was surrendered on 8th March, 1978. The service was incorporated into TGR 364/7, a daily service operating from Penybont to Carmarthen via Talog, Bwlchnewydd, Henfwlch and Trevaughan.

And a 'new' stage carriage licence application, submitted on 17th October 1979, was:-

TGR 364/12   Carmarthen (Bus Station) to Llanybri,
             via: Llanstephan and Llangain.   Monday to Saturday.
             This was merely a modification of TGR 364/11.   *Granted 9/1/1980.*

Three months later however, Des Jones asked for a modification to the above licence, to extend the journey on Wednesdays only, beyond Llanybri, to serve the neighbouring village of Llangynog, before returning to Carmarthen, via Alltycnap Road (a circular service). This modification was granted on 28th May, 1980.

In the meantime, a new Tory government embarked on a programme of deregulation and privatisation of bus services, and brought into being The Road Traffic Act (1980). The Act which came into effect on 1st October, 1980, allowed Express Carriage Services over 30 miles in distance to be freed from licensing regulations, and Excursions & Tours would not require licensing at all. Additionally, the restriction of advertising Excursions & Tours, which had previously applied to Ffoshelig Coaches, were lifted. The Act also abolished the licensing of bus conductors, and brought about the new 'coloured' operator licence discs. At the same time, operator licence numbers were changed from TGR xxx prefix, to PG xxx prefix (in the SWTA), with other traffic areas following suit with their own appropriate Traffic Area letters. The Transport Minister, Mr Norman Fowler, also announced that the 'New Bus Grant' scheme would cease by 31st March, 1984.

Simultaneously in 1980, Dyfed C.C. introduced a route numbering system for all stage carriage routes operating within the county. However, not many operators used their allocated route numbers until it became mandatory several years later. D. Jones & Sons, Ffoshelig Coaches, were amongst the group of late starters in 1990.

Above: **EMB 151K** was a 1972, Ford R226, with Plaxton 'Panorama Elite II' C53F coachwork, acquired in February 1980. It is seen here arriving at Queen Elizabeth Sec. School for girls, Llanstephan Rd, Carmarthen, to collect pupils for their homeward journey to Abernant. This coach passed to J.A. Evans, operator/dealer at Tregaron, in September 1982. *(V. Morgan collection).*

On 1st April, 1981, Des Jones applied for renewal of his 'O' licence with two modifications. The previous 'O' licence had been authorised to David Desmond Jones, trading as D. Jones & Sons, on operator reference number PG 364. The modifications asked for were a change of status from 'National' to 'International', and to include his wife's name, Irene May Jones.

This change of entity, however, warranted a new operator reference number, which became PG 5771, and was granted to D.D. & I.M. Jones, trading as D. Jones & Son in May 1981.

At the same time in May 1981, the four road service licences held by the company were issued with new PG numbers as follows:-

PG 364/5	**Abernant**	to **Carmarthen**	became PG 5771/1
PG 364/7	**Penybont**	to **Carmarthen**	became PG 5771/2
PG 364/10	**Trelech** (Sq)	to **Carmarthen**	became PG 5771/3
PG 364/12	**Carmarthen**	to **Llanybri**	became PG 5771/4
PG 364/11	**Carmarthen**	to **Llanybri**	was not renewed.

In due course, licences PG 364/5, 7, 10, 11, 12 were all surrendered.

Inevitably, March 1982, saw the arrival of the company's last 'grant aided' vehicle, in the form of a Ford R1114, with Plaxton 'Supreme VI' Express coachwork, pictured opposite.

Above: This Bedford VAS5, with Willowbrook B30F bodywork, **OBX 125J**, was acquired from Thomas Bros. Llangadog, Carmarthenshire, in January 1981. Thomas Bros. purchased it new in December 1970, with the aid of the 'New Bus Grant', and licensed it to their associate fleet 'LCW Motors' at Llandeilo, a business acquired by Thomas Bros. in November 1969. It was finally incorporated into the Thomas Bros fleet in January 1979, when all LCW licences were surrendered. It was captured here at Carmarthen Bus Station on lay over, before its return journey to Meidrim on Christmas eve 1986. OBX 125J, was a well maintained vehicle, and had three further owners after Ffoshelig Coaches, who sold it to Meurig's Coaches, (John Meurig Morgan, Lampeter), in October 1980, passing to J. Alwyn Evans, Tregaron, in March 1991, who sold it on to a private owner for caravan conversion. It was advertised for sale as a mobile caravan in 2010. *(V. Morgan).*

Above: Pictured here on lay-over at Carmarthen bus station on 31st October, 1984, is **VJU 259X**, a dealer registered Ford R1114, with 'grant specification' Plaxton 'Supreme VI Express' C53F coachwork. This happened to be the last 'grant aided' vehicle purchased by Ffoshelig Coaches, and arrived in March 1982, with a new style of livery. *(V. Morgan).*

Above: This Bedford YMT, **NBX 666R**, with Duple 'Dominant' C53F coachwork was purchased from Richards Bros. Cardigan, in February 1983, and operated in this Richards Bros' livery until it was bought back by Richards, in May 1983. *(V. Morgan).*

Above and opposite: Ffoshelig Coaches' publicity leaflet for the Llansteffan service in 1981.

ENJOY AN AFTERNOON ON LLANSTEFFAN BEACH OR VILLAGE GREEN
92p (children 61p)

The bus leaves the bus station, Blue Street, Carmarthen (stand 1) at 1.10 p.m. every day except Sunday. You arrive in Llansteffan at 1.30 p.m., and can then spend an afternoon watching cricket, exploring the castle or just relaxing on the beach. There's a bus back to Carmarthen at 5.10 p.m. which gets into the bus station at 5.30 p.m.

TWENTY MILES OF COAST AND COUNTRYSIDE
£1.00 (children 67p)

Why not enjoy a Wednesday round trip by bus? See Llangynog, Coombe Cheshire Home, Llanybri, Llansteffan and Llangain. Leave Carmarthen at 9.00 a.m. or 2.20 p.m., arrive back at 10.20 a.m. or 3.30 p.m.

		W		W		
Carmarthen	9.00	10.25	1.10	2.20	3.40	5.40
Llangain	9.10	10.35	1.20	-	3.50	5.50
Llansteffan	9.20	10.45	1.30	-	4.00	6.00
Llangynog	-	-	-	2.45	-	-
Llanybri	9.30	10.55	1.40	3.00	4.10	6.10
		W		W		
Llanybri	8.15	9.40	11.00	1.45	3.00	5.00
Llangynog	-	9.50	-	-	-	-
Llansteffan	8.25	-	11.10	1.55	3.05	5.10
Llangain	8.35	-	11.20	2.05	3.20	5.20
Carmarthen	8.55	10.20	11.30	2.15	3.30	5.30

CODE: W - Wednesday only

D. JONES & SON (FFOSHELIG COACHES)
Newchurch, Carmarthen.   Tel. Cynwil 211

Above and opposite: Ffoshelig Coaches' publicity leaflet for the Llansteffan service in 1981.

Above: Front cover of D. Jones & Son, Ffoshelig Coaches, July 1982, timetable.

224 TRELECH/MEIDRIM

		W	S	S	X WS
	a.m.	a.m.	a.m.	p.m.	p.m.
Trelech	8.00	10.00	10.30	1.00	4.45
Meidrim	8.25	10.25	10.55	1.25	5.05
Caerfyrddin Carmarthen	8.50	10.50	11.20	1.50	5.30

	WS	S	Th	X WS	
	a.m.	p.m.	p.m.	p.m.	p.m.
Caerfyrddin Carmarthen	9.15	12.00	1.30	4.00	5.45
Meidrim	9.40	12.25	1.55	4.25	6.10
Trelech	10.00	12.50	2.20	4.45	6.35

225 PENYBONT/BWLCHNEWYDD

		S	W	S	WS	X WS
	a.m.	a.m.	a.m.	p.m.	p.m.	p.m.
Penybont	8.00	—	10.10	12.00	—	4.50
Talog	8.25	—	10.25	12.25	—	5.15
Bwlchnewydd	8.35	10.20	10.35	12.35	1.50	5.25
Henfwlch	8.45	10.30	10.45	12.45	2.00	5.35
Caerfyrddin Carmarthen	9.00	10.45	11.00	1.00	2.15	5.50

	W	S	S	WS	S	X W	
	a.m.	a.m.	a.m.	p.m.	p.m.	p.m.	p.m.
Caerfyrddin Carmarthen	9.30	10.00	10.45	1.30	3.00	4.00	5.50
Henfwlch	9.45	10.15	11.00	1.45	3.15	4.15	6.05
Bwlchnewydd	9.50	10.20	11.05	1.50	3.20	4.20	6.10
Talog	10.00	—	11.15	—	3.30	4.30	6.20
Penybont	10.10	—	11.35	—	3.50	4.50	6.40

226 ABERNANT

Diwrnodau ysgol un unig   School days only

a.m.		p.m.
↑ 8.15	Abernant	↑ 4.35
8.35	Merthyr	4.15
8.40	Henfwlch	4.10
↓ 8.50	Caerfyrddin Carmarthen	4.00

Dydd Mercher yn unig	W	Wednesdays only
Dydd Sadwrn yn unig	S	Saturdays only
Hefyd yn rhadeg pob diwrnod ysgol	X	Also runs on all school days

DIM GWASANAETH A'R WYLIAU CENEDLAETHOL
NO SERVICE ON SUNDAYS OR BANK HOLIDAYS

Above: Page 2, of D. Jones & Son, Ffoshelig Coaches, July 1982, timetable.

223 MEIDRIM

	WS a.m.	WS p.m.
Meidrim	10.10	1.10
Caerfyrddin Carmarthen	10.35	1.45

	WS	S
Caerfyrddin Carmarthen	12.45	5.10
Meidrim	1.10	5.35

Jones Motors Ltd.
Isfryn
Login
Whitland

☎ Clunderwen 277

227 LLANYBRI/LLANSTEFFAN

	a.m.	W a.m.	a.m.	W p.m.	p.m.	p.m.
Llanybri	8.15	9.40	11.00	1.45	3.00	5.00
Llangynog	–	9.50	–	–	–	–
Llansteffan	8.25	–	11.10	1.55	3.05	5.10
Llangain	8.35	–	11.20	2.05	3.20	5.20
Caerfyrddin Carmarthen	8.55	10.20	11.30	2.15	3.30	5.30

	a.m.	W a.m.	p.m	W p.m.	p.m	p.m.
Caerfyrddin Carmarthen	9.00	10.25	1.10	2.20	3.40	5.40
Llangain	9.10	10.35	1.20	–	3.50	5.50
Llansteffan	9.20	10.45	1.30	–	4.00	6.00
Llangynog	–	–	–	2.45	–	–
Llanybri	9.30	10.55	1.40	3.00	4.10	6.10

SCENIC ROUTE

ENJOY AN AFTERNOON ON LLANSTEFFAN BEACH OR VILLAGE GREEN

£1.00 (children 66p)

The bus leaves the bus station, Blue Street, Carmarthen (stand 1) at 1.10 p.m. every day except Sunday. You arrive in Llansteffan at 1.30 p.m., and can then spend an afternoon watching cricket, exploring the castle or just relaxing on the beach. There's a bus back to Carmarthen at 5.10 p.m. which gets into the bus station at 5.30 p.m.

TWENTY MILES OF COAST AND COUNTRYSIDE

£1.06 (children 70p)

Why not enjoy a Wednesday round trip by bus? See Llangynog, Coombe Cheshire Home, Llanybri, Llansteffan and Llangain. Leave Carmarthen at 9.00 a.m. or 2.20 p.m., arrive back at 10.20 a.m. or 3.30 p.m.

Above: Page 3, of D. Jones & Son, Ffoshelig Coaches, July 1982. Timetable.

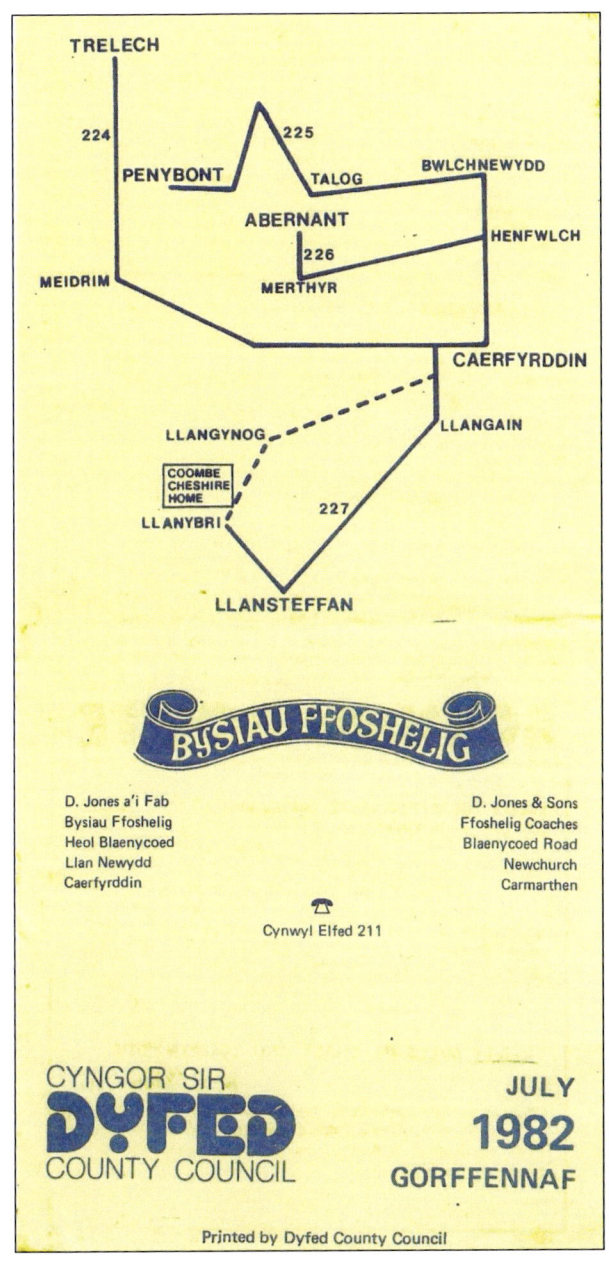

Above: Rear cover of D. Jones & Son, Ffoshelig Coaches, July 1982, timetable.

Above: This immaculate Leyland 'Leopard' PSU3C/4R, **VFH 700S**, with Duple 'Dominant' Express C53F coachwork was purchased from Pullham, Bourton-on-the-Water, Gloucestershire, in May 1983, to replace the Bedford YMT, NBX 666R, sold back to Richards Bros. Cardigan. **VFH 700S**, was one of the last few 'Dominant' Mk I built, and was a 'Grant Aided' vehicle new to Pullham in September 1977. Des Jones, 'Ffoshelig Coaches', sold this coach in September 1985, to Rees & Williams, Tycroes, and it passed to D Coaches, Morriston with the Rees & Williams business in August 1987. *(Vernon Morgan).*

Successful tendering for a Dyfed County Council supported service in August 1982, led to an application being submitted for the following stage carriage service licence:-

PG 5771/5 **Drefach** (C.P. School) to **Carmarthen** (Bus Station).
via: A48 to Blaenhirwaun and Garreg Hollt, unclassified road to Cefneithin, Foelgastell, Wig, Porthyrhyd Square, and A48 to Carmarthen.
Wednesdays only, 1 journey in each direction.
On journeys into Carmarthen, no passengers to be taken up after Wig, and on return from Carmarthen, no passenger to be dropped off before Wig.

The following 'licence for unforeseen service' was issued to operate the above service:-

PG 5771/Sp/1 **Drefach** (C.P. School) to **Carmarthen** (Bus Station)
period of operation 1/9/82 to 31/3/83

PG 5771/5 was granted 27/10/1982, with one condition: no local passengers to be conveyed between Drefach School and Cefneithin – to protect the services of South Wales Transport.

Above: The penultimate Bedford purchased by Des Jones, Ffoshelig, was **LTR 997R**, a Bedford YMT with Plaxton 'Supreme III' C53F coachwork, which arrived in August 1983, retaining the previous owner's livery until sold in April 1984. It's seen here at Carmarthen on 3rd March, 1984, working the Wednesday-only, Drefach to Carmarthen service. *(V. Morgan).*

Above: A nice rear end shot of Ford R1114, **VJU 259X**, and Volvo, **TNP 6X**, showing the welsh signwriting. Translated it reads: D. Jones and Son. Phone Conwil Elfed 211. Ffoshelig Coaches, Newchurch, Carmarthen. As for the Volvo, TNP 6X, Gwasanaeth Personol, means 'Personal Service'. This view was taken inside the new workshop, 15th May, 1985. *(V. Morgan).*

These two views of Des Jones (proprietor of Ffoshelig Coaches) behind the wheel of **TNP 6V** were taken at the depot on 15th May, 1985, when Des kindly brought it out of the garage to photograph. **TNP 6V** was a Volvo B58-56 with Caetano 'Alpha' C53F coachwork, purchased in May 1984, from Aston's Coaches, Kempsey, in who's livery it's seen here. Taking a liking to this livery, Des adopted it for the rest of the fleet. *(V. Morgan).*

Above: **STT 413R** was a Bristol LH6L with Eastern Coachworks B43F bodywork, acquired from Devon General O.C (121) in August 1984, and was new to Western National (121) in June 1977. This photograph was taken at Carmarthen in June 1985, before it was repainted into Jones' new livery of brown, cream and yellow. It passed to Rhodri Evans with the business in 1996.

Above: This Volvo B58-56, with Plaxton 'Supreme IV' Express C53F coachwork, **KUY 442X** was another coach purchased from Aston's, Kempsey, in September 1985, which passed to Rhodri Evans with the Ffoshelig business in 1996. *(V. Morgan).*

Above: Another view of the Volvo B58-56, **KUY 442X**, inside the original barn type garage building in 1986. *(V. Morgan).*

Above: The one and only mini-bus owned by Jones, Ffoshelig, was **D422 JDB**, a Freight Rover 350D with a Dixon-Lomas 'Made 2 Measure' conversion seating 16. It was acquired new in August 1986, and licensed 1st September. *(V. Morgan).*

THE EFFECTS OF DEREGULATION

Bus deregulation in Great Britain was set up in the Road Traffic Act (1985), introduced by the Conservative Government. The Act, scheduled to be implemented on 26th October, 1986, was basically the transfer of bus service operation from public bodies to private companies, as stipulated by the Act. It abolished 'Road Service Licensing' and allowed the introduction of competition on local bus services for the first time since 1931. To operate a service, all an accredited operator was required to do was to provide 56 days' notice to the Traffic Commissioner of their intention to commence, cease, or alter operation on a route.

The transition into deregulation, led by Transport Secretary, Nicholas Ridley, actually began on 6th January, 1986, with various provisions of the Act coming into force on that day:-

[A] The term 'Stage Carriage Service, changed to 'Local Service'.

[B] Licensing of 'Stage Carriage Services' abolished, changed to 'local service registration'.

[C] The term 'Express Carriage' was abolished.

[D] Requirement to notify 'Express Services' abolished.

From 1st March, 1986, the layout of 'Local Service Registration' (previously 'Stage Carriage' licensing) changed to a different format. The following registrations are in accordance with paragraph 10 of schedule 6, of the new Transport Act, and lists the local services that D.D. Jones & I.M. Jones trading as D. Jones & Son (Ffoshelig Coaches) registered with the Traffic Commissioners to commence with effect from 31st August, 1986. The registration was supported by Dyfed County Council, in accordance with *their* planned transition into deregulation of local bus services.

Dyfed C.C. gave the obligatory notice, and implemented the Road Traffic Act (1985), two months early, bringing in deregulation on 31st August, 1986, to coincide with the new academic year, the issuing of new school contracts, and renewal of tendered 'local services'.

Local services registered *before* 1st March 1986, by D.D. & I.M. Jones, t/a D. Jones & Son, to commence on 31st August, were mainly renewals of existing licences:-

PG 0091/5771   **Carmarthen** (Bus Station) to **Carmarthen** (Bus Station). *Route No.227* via: Johnstown, Llangain, Llanstephan and Llanybri.
Tuesday/Wednesday/Fridays only, two return journeys.
Previously PG 5771/4.   *S/deck operation, 56 seats or more.*
Modified 13/8/1986, diverting <u>into</u> Llangain village (Memorial Hall).

PG 0092/5771   **Carmarthen** (Bus Station) to **Carmarthen** (Bus Station). *Route No.219* via: Nantycaws, Llanddarog, Porthyrhyd, Drefach, Garreg Hollt, Cefneithin and Foelgastell.   *Wednesdays only, two return journeys.*
S/deck operation, 36-55 seats.

The remaining local services were not registered into the new system until 8th October 1986:-

PG 5076/5771 **Penybont** to **Carmarthen** (Bus Station). *Route No.225*
via: Talog, Bwlchnewydd, and Trevaughan. *Work and school journeys, plus shoppers service on some days.*
Monday to Saturday except B/H.
Normal stops. Hail & Ride. *S/deck operation, 36-55 seats.*

PG 5077/5771 **Ffoshelig Garage** to **Carmarthen** (Bus Station). *Route No.226*
via: Abernant, Merthyr and Trevaughan.
Schooldays only, one return journey.
Normal stops. Hail & Ride. *S/deck operation, 36-55 seats.*

PG 5078/5771 **Ffoshelig Garage** to **Llanybri**. *Route No.227*
via: Carmarthen bus station, Johnstown, Llangain and Llanstephan.
Monday to Saturday except B/H.
Normal stops. Hail & Ride. *S/deck operation, 36-55 seats.*

New local services registered 8th October 1986:-

PG 5079/5771 **Sarnau** to **Llanstephan Road Schools**. *Route No.228*
via: Llangynog and Carmarthen.
Schooldays only, one return journey.
Normal stops. Hail & Ride. *S/deck operation, 36-55 seats.*

PG 5080/5771 **Bryn Iwan** to **Llanstephan Road Schools**. *Route No.218*
via: Plasnewydd, Blaen-y-coed and Ffynnondrain.
Schooldays only, one return journey.
Normal stops. Hail & Ride. *S/deck operation, 36-55 seats.*

PG 5081/5771 **Llanfynydd** to **Carmarthen** (Bus Station). *Route No.240*
via: Court Henry, Dryslwyn, Llanarthney, Middleton Hall, and Capel-Dewi. *Saturdays only, two return journeys.*
Normal stops. Hail & Ride. *S/deck operation, 36-55 seats.*

On 6th May, 1987, D.D. & I.M. Jones, t/a D. Jones & Son, Ffoshelig Coaches, applied for renewal of their 'O' licence with a modification, for 1 mini-bus, and 10 single-deck vehicles. The Transport Manager was given as David Desmond Jones, the proprietor, with the operating centre (OC), registered as Ffoshelig Garage, Blaen-y-coed Road, Newchurch.

Renewal of the 'O' licence, PG 5771/SI was granted for the maximum permissible period of 5 years, a genuine reflection of the company's good repute.

Above: Former London Transport BL54, **OJD 54R**, was a Bristol LH6L with ECW B43F body acquired via Sworder, Walkern, East Hertfordshire, in March 1987. It's seen here outside Des Jones' house about to leave for Carmarthen on 23rd May, 1987. It served the business very well, passing to Edwards, Tiers Cross, Pembrokeshire, in June 1996, when Des decided to retire. After four further owners, it was sold for preservation in 2004, and is currently owned by a preservationist in the Cardiff area.
Below: Is another view of **OJD 54R**, the 7ft 6inch wide ECW bodied Bristol LH, which was captured on lay-over at Carmarthen, whilst operating the Dyfed C.C. supported service 227, to Llanstephan and Llanybri, on 4th April, 1992. *(V. Morgan).*

Above: Burry Port railway station, on 17th September, 1987, is the setting for this view of Jones, Ffoshelig's Volvo B10M-61, **A233 GNR**, with Duple 'Dominant IV' coachwork, down seated to C53F. It was the third Volvo purchased from Aston's of Kempsey, and arrived in January 1987. Incidentally, Towy Travel was a Llanfynydd based travel agent. *(V. Morgan).*

Above: Only one DAF chassis entered the Jones Ffoshelig fleet, and was pictured here at Carmarthen on 30th March, 1988. Dealer registered **E345 EVH**, it was a DAF MB230, with Duple 340, C55F coachwork, and arrived in September 1987, for the company's new holiday programme, which were discontinued after the coach was sold in March 1991. *(V. Morgan).*

Above: The first midi-bus in the fleet arrived in February 1988, as **E238 MBX**, a Mercedes-Benz 609D with Reeve Burgess B20F bodywork, and was purchased for the newly awarded Dyfed C.C. tendered operations listed on page 70, branded 'Town Link'. The four new daily Carmarthen town services were basically 'Hail & Ride' services, which brought passengers into the shopping centre, outside John Street Day Centre, (opposite Marks & Spencer), where this view was taken on 30th March, 1988.
Below: Is another view of E238 MBX, captured on stand No1 of Carmarthen bus station, working a quiet off-peak journey to Llanybri and Llanstephan, (service 227), on 25th March, 1989.   *(V. Morgan).*

Successful tendering to Dyfed C.C., for four completely new Carmarthen town services in early 1988, led to the purchase of a new Mercedes-Benz 609D, 20 seat mini-bus in February 1988, and the registration of four new local services commencing from 7th March 1988:-

PG 1794/5771 **Carmarthen** (John Street Day Centre) to **Cilddewi Park**.
via: Picton Terrace, Monument Hill, Glan Tawelan and Johnstown area.
No route number, but named Cilddewi Parc/Johnstown.
Monday – Saturday, except B/H.   *Normal stops and Hail & Ride.*
Commencing 7/3/1988.   S/deck operation, 17-35 seats.

PG 1795/5771 **Carmarthen** (John Street Day Centre) to **Penlan Rd/Capel Evan Rd.**
via: Penlan Rd, Parc-y-Delyn, Wellfield Rd, Llwyn Meredith, Courtlands Park, Parc-yr-Onnen, Francis Terrace, Capel Evan Road, Richmond Terrace.   *No route number, but named Penlan Rd/Capel Evan Rd.*
Monday – Saturday except B/H.   *Normal stops and Hail & Ride.*
Commencing 7/3/1988.   S/deck operation, 17-35 seats.

PG 1796/5771 **Carmarthen** (John Street Day Centre) to **Penlan/Ffos Rd.**
via: Ael-y-Bryn, Glynderi, Penlan, Ffos Rd, Abbey Mead, Priory St, and Richmond Terrace.   *No route number, but named Penlan/Ffos Road.*
Monday – Saturday, except B/H.   *Normal stops and Hail & Ride.*
Commencing 7/3/1988.   S/deck operation, 17-35 seats.

PG 1797/5771 **Carmarthen** (John Street Day Centre) to **Penymorfa**.
via: Penymorfa Lane, Awel Tywi, and Bryn Tywi.
No route number, but named Penymorfa.
Monday – Saturday, except B/H.   *Normal stops and Hail & Ride.*
Commencing 7/3/1988.   S/deck operation, 17-35 seats.

The above services were branded 'Town Link', together with another new local service gained through successful tendering a year later, in early 1989:-

PG 2193/5771 **Knightsford** to **Llanllwch Church**.
via: Ffoshelig, Ffynnonddrain, Nant-yr-Arian, Fountain Hall, and Alltycnap Road.   *No route number, but named Llanllwch.*
Wednesday only, 5 return journeys.   *Normal stops and Hail & Ride.*
Commencing 1/3/1989.   S/deck operation, 17-35 seats.

On 1st September, 1990, the four year term of Dyfed C.C. tendered operations ended, resulting in all operators having to re-tender for their services, and any other competing service they wished to operate – a situation brought about by deregulation. Complying with the law, and giving the obligatory notice, Des Jones cancelled all of his tendered service licences, PG 1794 to 1797/5771, from 20/7/90, PG 2193/5771 from 31/8/90, whilst PG 5075 to 5081 and PG 0091/5771 were cancelled from 2/9/90. The licences would then only be renewed, after successfully regaining the services.

Consequently, the local authority made major changes to the network of contracted local bus services, and introduced the title 'BWS DYFED' (Dyfed Bus), to the unit responsible for the operation of all supported services.

At the same time, the privatised South Wales Transport Company (SWT), by then owned by 'Badgerline Holdings', deviously undercut tenders submitted by the established operators of south-east Dyfed, which included Jones, Ffoshelig. Under these circumstances, Ffoshelig Coaches lost their long standing services, Carmarthen to Meidrim and Trelech (224), and Carmarthen to Penybont and Trelech (225), resulting in loss of revenue.

Losing that work was a big worry to the Jones family, and as a direct result, Des Jones' son Rhydian, saw no future in the bus industry, and joined the police force.

Seeking alternative work for the business, Des Jones introduced a British holiday tours programme, which included all the popular destinations.

However, the company successfully received alternative work in the 1990 round of local authority tenders, which were registered as follows:-

PG 2782/5771 **Carmarthen (Bus Station) to Carmarthen (Bus Station).** *Route 228*
via: Pass By, Sarnau, Llangynog Hall, Alltycnap Road, and Johnstown.
At first no route number, but later numbered 228. 'Town Link' service. Wednesdays only, 2 return journeys. Normal stops and Hail & Ride. Commencing 5/9/1990. S/deck operation 36-55 seats.

PG 2783/5771 **Ffoshelig Garage to Johnstown Schools (Llanstephan Rd).** *Route 226*
via: Abernant, Rickett's Mill, Merthyr Junction, Henfwlch, Trevaughan, Carmarthen, and Llanstephan Rd.
Schooldays only, morning and afternoon. Normal stops and Hail & Ride. Commencing 3/9/1990. S/d operation, 36-55 seats.

PG 2874/5771 **Carmarthen (Bus Station) to Nant-Yr-Arian.** *Route No.240*
via: Fountain Hall Terrace. *Monday – Friday, 3 daily journeys.*
'Town Link' service. Normal stops and Hail & Ride. Commencing 3/9/1990. S/deck operation, 36-55 seats.

PG 2875/5771 **Blaen-y-coed Rd (Ffoshelig Garage) to Carmarthen Schools.**
Route No.224
via: Maniwan, Trelech, Meidrim, Pass By, Carmarthen (bus Station), Bro-Myrddyn and Llanstephan Road schools. *Normal stops. Hail & Ride. Schooldays only, 1 return journey.*
Commencing 3/9/1990. S/deck operation, 36-55 seats.

PG 2876/5771 **Blaen-y-coed Rd (Ffoshelig Garage)** to **Johnstown Sch**. *Route No.225*
via: Penybont, Groesffordd, Talog, Bwlchnewydd and Carmarthen.
School or works service, Monday – Saturday, 1 return journey.
School service, 2 return journeys except B/H. Normal stops, Hail & Ride.
Commencing 3/9/1990. S/deck operation, 36-55 seats.

PG 2877/5771 **Bryn Iwan** to **Carmarthen (Johnstown Schools)**. *Route No.219*
via: Blaen-y-coed, Carmarthen Golf Club, Ffoshelig, Ffynnonddrain, Carmarthen Town and Llanstephan Road. *Normal stops, Hail & Ride.*
Schooldays only, 1 return journey.
Commencing 3/9/1990. S/deck operation, 56 seats or more.

PG 2878/5771 **Carmarthen (Bus Station)** to **Llangynog (Hall)**. *Route No.228*
via: Sarnau, Llangynog (Hall), Cwrt Malle, Alltycnap Road, Johnstown, Brewery Road, Llanstephan Road Schools. *Normal stops. Hail & Ride.*
Schooldays only, 1 return journey.
Commencing 3/9/1990. S/deck operation, 56 seats or more.

PG 2880/5771 **Carmarthen (Bus Station)** to **Llanybri**. *Route No.227*
via: Johnstown, Llangain, Llanstephan and Llanybri. *Monday - Saturday, 5 return journeys daily incl. Good Friday. Normal stops. Hail & Ride.*
Commencing 3/9/1990. S/deck operation, 36-55 seats.

<u>Above:</u> Former Inter Valley Link (23) **UKG 423S**, was a Leyland Leopard PSU3E/2R with Willowbrook B51F bodywork, purchased from Davies Bros (Pencader) Ltd, in July 1990, to operate the 227 Llanybri service mentioned above, but is pictured here at the Llanstephan Road Schools, on 13th September 1991, working school service 219, to Blaen-y-coed.   *(V. Morgan).*

PG 2892/5771   **Carmarthen (Bus Station)** to **Knightsford**.   *Route No.244*
              via: Lime Grove, Ffynnonddrain and Ffoshelig.   *'Town Link' service.*
              2 return journeys, Wednesdays only.   Normal stops, and Hail & Ride.
                      Commencing 5/9/1990. S/deck operation, 36-55 seats.

PG 2893/5771   **Penymorfa (Awel Tywi)** to **Penymorfa (Awel Tywi)**. *Route No.241/2*
              via: Penymorfa Lane, Carmarthen bus station, Johnstown, Cilddewi Park.
              2 return journeys, Monday – Friday, except B/H.   'Town Link' service.
              Penymorfa – 241, Cilddewi Park – 242. Normal stops and Hail & Ride.
                      Commencing 3/9/1990. S/deck operation, 17-35 seats.

These Dyfed C.C. sponsored 'Town Link' services were in their experimental stage at this point, which explains the numerous changes since the original routes appeared in March 1988. The 'Town Link' services were the basis of what eventually became the Carmarthen 'Dial-a-ride' services in 1998.

In early 1991, another new 'Town Link' service was successfully gained by Des Jones:-

PG 3105/5771   **Carmarthen (Bus Station)** to **Glynderi**.   *Route No.243*
              via: Abbey Mead, Aelybryn, Glynderi and Penlan Ffos Road.
              2 return journeys, Tuesdays/Fridays only. Normal stops and Hail & Ride.
                      Commencing 9/4/1991. S/deck operation, 17-35 seats.

Above: This very tidy Duple 'Dominant' B53F bodied Leyland 'Leopard', **MPG 153P**, was new to 'Safeguard' of Guildford in 1976, but was acquired from Jenkins, Capel Iwan, Newcastle Emlyn, when Jenkins ceased operating in July 1991. *(V. Morgan).*

Above: C826 CBU was a Dodge S56 with Northern Counties B18F bodywork, acquired from Greater Manchester Buses (1826), in October 1991, for the Dyfed C.C., (Bws Dyfed) contracted 'Town Link' network of services. It is pictured here leaving Carmarthen bus station on 4th December, 1991, working one of the 'Town Link' services, 242 to Cilddewi Park, which is situated on the western fringes of the town. The route was Carmarthen bus station, Lammas Street, Johnstown, Cilddewi Park, Parc-y-ffordd, and Carmarthen (BS) circular. The Bws Dyfed sign was a specific requirement for the tendered contract. *(V. Morgan).*

Above: Another view of the Dodge S56, **C826 CBU**, at the original Carmarthen bus station, 18th April, 1994, still displaying its Greater Manchester fleet number. The branding on the off-side reads, 'Jones Ffoshelig, 1921-1991, Going Long – Going Strong', and the near side was lettered with the wesh equivelent, 'Mynd o's 'spel – a dal i fynd'. *(V. Morgan collection).*

Above: This Volvo B58-56, **XUY 59V**, with Plaxton 'Supreme IV' Express C53F coachwork, was the last coach purchased by Des Jones in March 1992. It was acquired from D.R. Morris, Bromyard, bearing its fifth registration number, and is seen here at Trimsaran on 20th July, 1992, after receiving a chassis cleaning pressure wash at Davies Bros' Trimsaran depot. *(V. Morgan).*

On 18th March 1992, the company asked for renewal of their 'O' licence, PG 5771/SI, which was granted for the maximum period of 5 years, on 28th May 1992. The transport manager was given as David Desmond Jones, with authorisation for 11 single-deck vehicles.

However, when the local authority tendered services expired on 3rd September, 1994, the following Bws Dyfed services were cancelled accordingly:-

PG 0092/5771, PG 2782/5771 and PG 2892/5771 from 31/8/1994.

PG 2874/5771, PG 2893/5771 and PG 3105/5771 from 2/9/1994.

PG 2875/5771, PG 2876/5771 and PG 2880/5771 from 3/9/1994.

The four school services were not cancelled, as their contracts continued, and in August 1994, the following services were awarded by Dyfed C.C., and registered accordingly:-

PG 4223/5771   **Carmarthen (Bus Station)** to **Llanybri**.   *Route No.227*
                via: Johnstown, Llangain and Llanstephan.   *'Town Link' service.*
                A reduced service to 2 journeys daily, on Tue/Wed/Fri only.
                (SWT gained the main daily Monday – Saturday services).
                Normal stops and Hail & Ride.   *Operated on behalf of Bws Dyfed.*
                Commencing 6/9/1994. S/deck operation, 36-55 seats.

PG 4224/5771 **Carmarthen (Bus Station)** to **Glynderi.** *Route No.243*
via: Spilman Street, Abbey Mead, Ael-y-bryn and Glynderi.
Tuesday & Friday only, 2 journeys per day. *'Town Link' service.*
Normal stops and Hail & Ride. *Operated on behalf of Bws Dyfed.*
Commencing 6/9/1994. S/deck operation, 17-35 seats.

PG 4225/5771 **Carmarthen (Bus Station)** to **Llwynmeredydd.** *Route No.245*
via: Priory Street, Old Oak Lane, and Capel Evan Road.
Service operated jointly with Davies Bros, and South Wales Transport.
Monday to Saturday, 1 journey per day, per operator.
Operated on behalf of Bws Dyfed. *'Town Link' service.*
Normal stops and Hail & Ride.
Commencing 5/9/1994. S/deck operation, 17-35 seats.

PG 4226/5771 **Carmarthen (Bus Station)** to **Nant yr Arian** *Route No.240*
via: Fountain Hall.
Monday to Saturday, 2 journeys per day. *'Town Link' service.*
Normal stops and Hail & Ride. *Operated on behalf of Bws Dyfed.*
Commencing 5/9/1994. S/deck operation, 17-35 seats.

PG 4227/5771 **Carmarthen (Bus Station)** to **Penymorfa.** *Route No.241*
via: Awel Tywi and Bryn Tywi.
Monday to Friday, 2 journeys per day. *'Town Link' service.*
Normal stops and Hail & Ride. *Operated on behalf of Bws Dyfed.*
Commencing 5/9/1994. S/deck operation, 17-35 seats.

PG 4228/5771 Registered as **Ffoshelig Garage** to **Johnstown Schools.** *Route No.225*
It was actually Talog to Carmarthen and Johnstown Schools.
via: American House, Talog, Groesffordd, Penybont, Bwlchnewydd, Henfwlch, Carmarthen bus station, extending to Ysgol Bro Myrddin, and Llanstephan Road Schools on school days only.
Mondays to Saturdays. Local service and school service.
Normal stops and Hail & Ride. *Operated on behalf of Bws Dyfed.*
Commencing 5/9/1994. S/deck operation, 56 seats or more.

PG 4229/5771 Registered as **Ffoshelig Garage** to **Johnstown Schools.** *Route No.224*
It was actually Trelech to Carmarthen and Johnstown Schools.
via: Trelech, Groesffordd, Meidrim, Pass By, Carmarthen bus station, Ysgol Bro Myrddin and Llanstephan Road Schools on school days only.
Local service and school service. *Mondays to Saturdays.*
Normal stops and Hail & Ride. *Operated on behalf of Bws Dyfed.*
Commencing 5/9/1994. S/deck operation, 56 seats or more.

Above: Pictured here outside Ffoshelig Garage on 27th May, 1996, about to depart for Carmarthen, is **GMS 305S**, a former Kelvin Scottish, 1978 Leyland 'Leopard' PSU3E/4R with Alexander 'Y type' B53F bodywork, acquired from Henley's, Abertillery, in October 1994. This vehicle passed to Lewis, Whitland, with part of the Ffoshelig business, on 1st June, 1996. *(V. Morgan).*

Above: The last vehicle purchased by Des Jones, Ffoshelig, in October 1994, was **M794 MTH**, a new Mercedes-Benz 709D, with Mellor B27F bodywork, which is seen here departing from Carmarthen bus station on 14th February, 1995, working one of the 'Bws Dyfed' tendered 'Town Link' services, 241 to Penymorfa, on the south-east fringes of town. *(V. Morgan).*

Ten stressful years after the introduction of deregulation, Des Jones decided to retire from the business, coinciding with the company's 75th anniversary in 1996. His son, Rhydian chose not to take over the business, as he had settled into his new career as a police officer. Consequently, the business was offered for sale.

It was thought that Dewi Davies, managing director of the Davies Bros. group of companies, at Pencader, Carmarthen, and Trimsaran, would have absorbed the business, as he had a penchant for acquiring local omnibus businesses – but on this occasion, he did not.

The mystery unfolded a few months later, when Davies Bros. started slimming down their business, selling all nine local services operated from the Trimsaran base, to competitors First Bus PLC., for their subsidiary, South Wales Transport, at the same time closing down and eventually selling off their Trimsaran premises.

More information on the activities of Davies Bros., can be found in my publication 'Davies Bros. [Pencader] Ltd.' available at www.vernonmorgan.com

There were no offers to buy 'Ffoshelig' as a complete unit, so the business was divided into three parts, and sold off individually. The 'Town Link' services 240/1/3/5, and local services 224/5, together with one Mercedes-Benz midi-bus, M794 MTH, passed to Castle Garages of Llandovery. Elfed Lewis of Whitland, acquired the school journeys of service 224/5, and the local service 227, together with three vehicles, Volvo B10M, A233 GNR, and Leyland 'Leopard' buses MPG 153P / GMS 305S, on 3rd June, 1996. The largest part of the Ffoshelig business, three vehicles, three school contracts, 219, 226/8, tours and private hire, together with the trading name, goodwill, and telephone number, passed to Rhodri Evans, a former part-time driver at Ffoshelig.

Phillip Rhodri Evans, was not a newcomer to the coach business. He had already commenced coach operating nine months earlier, in September 1995, from the family's farm at Maes-y-Prior, St. Peters, Carmarthen. However, maintenance facilities at Maes-y-Prior were inadequate for the larger fleet, resulting in the lease of Ffoshelig Garage from the Jones family, which became Rhodri Evans' new operating centre from 3rd June, 1996.

It must be noted that Des Jones' standards in the bus and coach business were second to none. His vehicles were always presented in a professional manner, and always in immaculate condition - a tradition that has passionately continued with the current owner of Ffoshelig Coaches, Rhodri Evans.

This leads me to mention a particular incident which occurred in late 1989, when a Davies Bros. bus collided with one of Ffoshelig's coaches at the Queen Elizabeth Cambria School, bus bays, in Llanstephan Road, Carmarthen. During the several weeks of repair to Ffoshelig's coach, Davies Bros. provided a replacement coach LBX 861P, which returned to Pencader in pristine condition, inside and outside – like brand new!

Above: This heavily disguised Bedford YRQ, with Duple 'Dominant I' body, was new to D. Jones, Ffoshelig Coaches, in April 1974, as **XTH 700M,** and was sold by Des Jones in July 1984, for export to Malta. It arrived in Malta, August 1984, passing to E. Galea, of Gzira, north of Valetta - the capital of Malta, entering service in November 1984, as Y-1112. Quickly re-registered Y- 0411, it was finally re-registered DBY- 411, as pictured here at Qawra bus station in 2009. Following a replacement Bedford engine, it received a Perkins 6.354 engine, and finally a DAF power unit in May 2008. The vehicle was extensively refurbished in 2005, following an accident, which included fitting new reclining coach seats. The coach seats were replaced by bus seats in 2009, as shown. At the start of July 2011, it passed to Transport Malta, after 'Route Bus' operation finished, and quickly passed to Tar-Robba, for scrapping, with formal documentation of its scrapping being issued in October 2011.

I am indebted to John Bennett, for the use of this photograph and information.

On 5th June, 1996, the following message appeared in a local newspaper:-

'Omnibus Vote of Thanks'

"Nearing retirement from the bus and coach industry, we wish to record our sincere thanks to customers for loyal support on our local services, day tours and private hire.

We especially wish to thank the thousands of school pupils, many of whom by now have their own children travelling on Ffoshelig buses, for the immense pleasure they have given us over the years.

And a big thank you to our drivers for looking after our patrons so well, and for driving our vehicles in a competent, sympathetic and professional manner. We will really miss you boys.

We record our appreciation to officers of the transportation and education departments, for their valued assistance, advice, and support, so readily and pleasantly made available to us.

Thanks also to friends and colleagues in the industry for readily helping us.

Our best wishes to these and the three operators taking over our business – Mr Rhodri Evans, Ffoshelig Garage, Jones Bros., Castle Garage, Llandovery, and Mr Elfed Lewis of Whitland.

Finally, thank you to the very large number of people who have offered assistance to us over the years, farmers for towing our buses from snow drifts, shoppers for relaying vital messages, parents for fully supporting us on matters of discipline etc.

You are too numerous to name, but too important to forget".

Diolch o gallon I bawb. **Des and Irene Jones, Bysiau Ffoshelig.**

FFOSHELIG COACHES UNDER NEW OWNERSHIP

When Desmond Jones retired in June 1996, 'Ffoshelig Coaches' was divided into three parts, and sold off individually, as stated on page 78. The largest portion, together with the trading name and goodwill, passed to Phillip Rhodri Evans of Carmarthen.

Rhodri was not a newcomer to the coach industry, having previously worked at Davies Bros (Pencader) Ltd, Lewis, Whitland, and Ffoshelig Coaches, before starting his own business in September 1995. His first licence application for the use of 2 single-deck vehicles in June 1995, was heard at a public inquiry, held at Carmarthen District Council Offices, Spilman St., Carmarthen, on 22nd August, 1995, and was granted as applied for on PG 6927/SN, trading as 'Rhodri Evans'. The OC was given as the family's farm, 'Maes-y-Prior', Llysonnen Road, St. Peters, Carmarthen, and the Transport Manager Phillip Rhodri Evans.

In February 1996, the authorisation for two single deck vehicle licences was modified to International status, becoming PG 6927/SI, and in April 1996, two additional single deck licences were applied for, in readiness for the proposed partial takeover of Ffoshelig. At the same time, the proposed 'Ffoshelig' school services were registered:-

PG 4644/6927 **Abernant** to **Carmarthen (Llanstephan Rd. Schools)**. *Route No.226*
via: Ricketts Mill, Henfwlch, Trevaughan and Carmarthen Town.
School service, schooldays only, 1 inward, & 1 outward journey per day.
Normal stops and Hail & Ride. *Commencing 3/6/1996.*

PG 4645/6927 **Sarnau** to **Carmarthen (Llanstephan Rd. Schools)**. *Route No.228*
via: Llangynog, Alltycnap Road and Johnstown.
School service, schooldays only, 1 inward, & 1 outward journey per day.
Normal stops, and Hail & Ride. *Commencing 3/6/1996.*

PG 4646/6927 **Bryn Iwan** to **Carmarthen (Llanstephan Rd. Schools)**. *Route No.219*
via: Blaen-y-coed, Carmarthen Golf Club, Ffynnonddrain & Carmarthen.
School service, schooldays only, 1 inward, & 1 outward journey per day.
Normal stops, and Hail & Ride. *Commencing 3/6/1996.*

After registering the additional licences in May 1996, Rhodri Evans took full control of the Ffoshelig business, from Monday 3rd June, 1996, operating with his own licence discs, PG 6927/SI, from Ffoshelig Garage, Newchurch, which was leased from the Jones family. From that date, Ffoshelig Garage was registered as P.R. Evans' new operating centre, but it was not until February 1997, that his licence was modified to use the trading name of 'Ffoshelig Coaches'. Concurrently, authorisation was granted to increase the vehicle licence discs to seven single-deck vehicles, and as the business expanded, was increased to eight single-deck vehicles in October 1999. Initially, there was very little noticeable difference to the Ffoshelig vehicles, but subtle changes have been introduced as time has passed. Nevertheless, the superb livery of mid-cream and brown has been retained.

Above: Rhodri Evans' first vehicle after gaining his operator licence in August 1995, was this Volvo B58-56, with Plaxton 'Supreme IV' C53F coachwork, retrofitted with a Plaxton 'Paramount' front end. Purchased from J.A. Evans, Tregaron, it was new to Wallace Arnold, Leeds, in April 1980, as *LUA 254V*, and had been re-registered **YMU 134** by a previous owner. It returned to Evans, Tregaron, in January 1996, in part exchange for the DAF pictured below. *(Courtesy of Rhodri Evans).*

Above: B665 OFP was a DAF SB2300, with Plaxton 'Paramount 3200' C53F coachwork, and is seen here at King Edward VII Avenue, Cardiff, on 17th February, 1996, carrying the livery of a previous owner, Owen of Nefyn, North Wales. It was acquired in January 1996, from David Clive Edwards, Whitland, who later became Taf Valley Coaches (Bysiau Cwm Taf), but purchased via J.Alwyn Evans, an operator and dealer at Tregaron, Ceredigion. *(V. Morgan collection).*

Above: This very tidy Bristol LH6L, with ECW B43F body, **STT413R**, passed to Rhodri Evans with the Ffoshelig business in June 1996. The only outwardly change to this vehicle was the legal lettering, and is seen here at Carmarthen, between journeys on the 226 school service to Abernant, on 18th July, 1997. It passed to Rapson, Brora, Scotland, in October 1997. *(V. Morgan).*

Above: KUY 442X also passed to Rhodri Evans on 3rd June, 1996 with the Ffoshelig business. This Volvo B58-56 with Plaxton 'Supreme IV' coachwork was sold to J. Alwyn Evans (dealer/operator) Tregaron, in April 2001, and on to Keith Jones (Travel Final) Blaengarw, Mid-Glam in April 2001. *(V. Morgan collection).*

Above: The third vehicle transferred to Rhodri Evans with the purchase of Jones, Ffoshelig's business in June 1996, was this Volvo B58-61, **XUY 59V**, with Plaxton 'Supreme IV' coachwork, which again, retained the 'Jones' lettering until it was sold to Clive Edwards (Taf Valley Coaches) Whitland, in May 1997. *(V. Morgan).*

Above: In September 1996, the DAF pictured on page 82, B665 OFP, was part exchanged for two 1982 Leyland 'Tigers'. Seen here at King Edward VII Avenue, Cardiff, on 1st February 1997, is one of the pair, **ARR 956Y** which was new as *VRA 3Y*, to Derby C.T. This was a TRCTL11/3R model, with Plaxton 'Supreme V' coachwork, which had received a Plaxton 'Paramount' front end by a previous owner. It was purchased by Rhodri Evans, and lettered as 'Jones Ffoshelig'. *(V. Morgan).*

Above: This Leyland 'Tiger' TRCTL11/2R, **NDW 147X**, with Plaxton 'Supreme VI Express' coachwork, is the other 'Tiger' mentioned opposite as purchased with ARR 956Y, in a deal with Mid-West Coach Sales, August 1996. New to Hill's, Tredegar in March 1982, it left the Ffoshelig stable after one month, passing to Thomas & Pugh, Upper Tumble. *(V. Morgan collection).*

Above: Former Merthyr Tydfil 229, **JUH 229W**, a Leyland 'Leopard' PSU4F/2R, with Duple 'Dominant' B47F body, was acquired in November 1996, after a brief period of 2 months with Williams, Porthcawl. It is pictured here on 13th May, 1997, at the Llanstephan Road schools, Carmarthen, working service 226 to Abernant, in the livery of Jones, Login, where it had spent 7 years after leaving Merthyr. A former Jones, Ffoshelig, 'Leopard', GMS 305S, owned by Lewis, Whitland, is visible in the backdrop, and is working service 225 to Penybont, a service Lewis acquired from Jones Ffoshelig in June 1996. *(V. Morgan).*

Above: Another view of the former Merthyr Tydfil B.C., Duple 'Dominant' bodied 'Leopard', **JUH 229W**, captured at Carmarthen railway station on 9th October, 1997, shows it in fleet livery, and converted to B53F with 3+2 seating. *(V. Morgan).*

Above: Yet another view of the former Merthyr Tydfil Leyland 'Leopard', JUH 229W, with Rhodri Evans, 'Ffoshelig Coaches', seen after losing its destination box and a repaint into yellow 'School Bus' livery. In March 2000, it was re-seated to DP45F, specification, fitted with 45 second-hand coach seats. This vehicle passed to Silver Star, Caernarfon, in July 2005.

Above: This Volvo B10M-61, with Plaxton 'Paramount 3200' C53F coachwork, was purchased from Bernard Hillman of Tredegar, with the cherished registration **DSU 772**, in May 1997. It was new to Excelsior, Bournemouth, as *B908 SPR* in April 1985, and was rebuilt with a 'Paramount III' front end by its third owner, Hillman. It operated in this livery for several months, and is shown **Below:** re-painted into fleet livery, up-seated to C57F and re-registered with another cherished plate **RAZ 9859** in April 1998. The DSU 772 registration was then transferred to another Volvo in the fleet. *(**Above:** Courtesy of Rhodri Evans.)*
*(**Below:** V. Morgan).*

Above: This Leyland 'Leopard' PSU5D/4R, with Plaxton 'Supreme IV' C57F coachwork was new to National Travel (West) 268, registered *MRJ 268W*, in November 1980. It later passed to Goodwin, Eccles, Gtr. Manchester, where it received a cherished registration, *WSV 550*, and passed to Edwards, Tiers Cross, Pembrokeshire in September 1996 as *SVM 475W*. Edwards immediately re-registered it with cherished registration **WJB 490**. When Rhodri purchased this coach from Edwards in August 1997, it was agreed that the registration mark would be returned, but the coach was painted and lettered before that actually happened. It was re-registered **GDE 416W** by Rhodri Evans in August 1997, as shown in the photograph below.
Below: **GDE 416W** (*WJB 490*) is seen here at Carmarthen railway station on 21st September, 1997.   (V. Morgan).

Above: Another vehicle purchased from Bernard Hillman, Tredegar, complete with the cherished registration, was this Volvo B10M-61, **JIL 2433**, *(previously KXI 366, NGT 1Y)*, with Plaxton 'Paramount 3500' C49FT coachwork that had been modernised with a 'Paramount Mk III' front end. It had been new to Richmond, Epsom, in March 1983, and arrived at 'Ffoshelig' in August 1997, and pressed into service still wearing Hillman's (White Lion Coaches) livery, as shown in October 1997. *(VM)*.
Below: Is another view of **JIL 2433**, which is seen here on 23rd February, 1998, looking really smart in the 'Ffoshelig' livery, and passed to closely associated, Davies Coaches, Llanelli, in March 2001. *(V. Morgan)*.

BYSIAU FFOSHELIG,
HEOL BLAENYCOED,
CAERFYRDDIN.
SA33 6EG

FFOSHELIG COACHES,
BLAENYCOED ROAD,
CARMARTHEN.
SA336EG

Established 1921

Bysiau FFOSHELIG Coaches

Proprietor : Rhodri Evans
STANDARD & EXECUTIVE COACHES

TELEPHONE/FAX: (01267) 281211

Above: A business card for Ffoshelig Coaches dated 1998 - after Rhodri Evans had taken control of the business.

Above: When this Volvo B10M-61, with Plaxton 'Paramount 3500 Mk III' coachwork arrived from Moffat & Williamson, Gauldry, Scotland, in April 1998, it was registered *E565 UHS*. That registration mark was immediately replaced by a cherished registration, **DSU 772**, removed from an earlier Volvo B10M in the fleet, and is seen here at Carmarthen railway station car park, on 30th September, 1998. Visible in the backdrop is part of Carmarthen town and the Castle ruins, dating from the 1100s. The high wall immediately behind the coach is a flood defence for the river Towy. *(V. Morgan).*

Above: It will be noticed throughout this publication that Rhodri Evans has a penchant for cherished registration marks. This 1982 Leyland 'Leopard' PSU3G/4R, with Plaxton 'Supreme IV Express' coachwork, was acquired from Mayne, of Clayton, Manchester, complete with its cherished registration, **LIL 9924**, in August 1998. Previously registered *VRC 610Y*, it was sold to Morris Travel, Carmarthen in November 2000, together with its cherished registration. *(V. Morgan).*

June 1999, saw the sudden and unexpected collapse of Davies Bros (Pencader) Ltd, which were by then based in new premises at Dolgwili Road, Carmarthen.

A detailed history of Davies Bros' business is available at: www.vernonmorgan.com

After the sale of Davies Bros' main business to First Bus Group, several surplus buses and coaches were auctioned by the receivers, in a sale at Pencader, August 1999. At this sale, Rhodri Evans bought two elderly Leyland 'Leopard' coaches, but sold them on without operating them. One was immediately sold to Kenneth Alun Davies, Rhodri's engineer, who applied for his own operator licence, and having good rapport with Rhodri, commenced operations from the same rented premises. Two months later in October 1999, Rhodri Evans was granted a licence variation, to increase the vehicle licence authorisation from seven single-deck vehicles to eight, from the same address at Blaen-y-coed Road, Carmarthen SA33 6EG. At the same time, the main operating centre remained as Blaen-y-coed Road, Carmarthen, but an additional operating centre was registered as Maes-y-prior, Llysonnen Road, Carmarthen SA33 5DS – Rhodri Evans' original operating centre, at his home address. The Transport Manager was recorded as Phillip Rhodri Evans, the proprietor.

Above: **V2 FOS** was the first 'new' vehicle purchased by Rhodri Evans in September 1999. It was a 12 metre Dennis Javelin, with Berkhof 'Axial 50' C51FT coachwork. It's pictured here at King Edward VII Avenue, Cardiff on 20th May, 2000, working a private hire assignment. It was re-registered V35 LDE in January 2001, and sold. See below. *(V. Morgan).*

Above: This photograph of **V35 LDE**, *previously V2 FOS* was taken on the day it left Ffoshelig Coaches in January 2001, for Isaac & Morgan (G&M Coaches) Lampeter. It did not operate with Ffoshelig on this registration mark. *(Rhodri Evans).*

Above: **JTU 229T** was a Bedford YRQ, with Plaxton 'Supreme IV' C45F body, acquired from J.M. Morgan, (Meurig's Coaches) Lampeter, in Sept. 1998. It operated a few school journeys before being dismantled for spares, and sold for scrap.   *(V. M).*

Above: This much travelled Leyland 'Tiger', **JUI 1720**, with Plaxton 'Supreme V' C53F coachwork, arrived from Taf-Valley Coaches, Whitland, in November 1999, and operated in this livery for 6 months. It's seen in fleet livery next page. *(V. Morgan).*

Above: Leyland 'Tiger' **JUI 1720** received fleet livery in May 2000, when it was re-seated to C57F. This one passed to Morris Travel, Carmarthen in February 2002, where it eventually returned to its original registration mark, *UPG 349X*.

Above: This 1987 Volvo B10M-61, with Plaxton 'Paramount 3500' C51F coachwork, **KUI 1372**, was acquired from Taf-Valley Coaches, Whitland, in May 2000, and is seen on layover at Carmarthen railway station on 21st November, 2000. It was the first vehicle in the fleet to receive vinyl lettering, opposed to hand sign writing, although some were still sign written later. *(V.M)*.

In May 2000, Rhodri Evans decided to expand his sphere to include a local service, and registered the following service which had been abandoned by First Bus Group, after their absorption of Davies Bros (Pencader) Ltd., business, previously route numbers 202/209:-

PG 7242/6927   **Johnstown** (Davies' Estate) to **Glangwili Hospital** (Gates).   *Route No 210*
via: Carmarthen Bus Station.   *Mondays – Fridays only.*
Normal stops.   Commencing 2/5/2000.

The above service was cancelled from 7/7/2000, due to lack of support, and a short while later, a school service was registered as a local service:-

PG 7523/6927   **Davies' Estate** (Johnstown) to **Johnstown C.P. School**.   *Route No 249*
via: Llanstephan Road.
To operate Monday – Friday, only when Johnstown C.P. School is open.
Normal stops.   Commencing 14/11/2000.

PG 7523/6927   above was un-remunerative and cancelled from 2/2/2001.

Above: **A10 SBK** was a Leyland 'Tiger' TRCL10/3ARZM, with a Cummins L10 engine, and Plaxton 'Paramount 3500' Mk III, C49FT coachwork, which was new as *E510 RFU*, to municipal operator, Grimsby-Cleethorpes Transport (180), in June 1988. It operated in the livery of Peter Sheffield, a subsidiary of GCT, and received cherished registration *PS 2743*, which was removed and re-registered *E882 HFW* upon sale to Swanbrook of Cheltenham. Swanbrook, gave it cherished registration **A10 SBK**, which remained on the coach when sold to Meurig Morgan, Lampeter, in May 1997, later passing to his daughter, trading as G & M Coaches, Lampeter, before arriving at Ffoshelig Coaches in January 2001, still wearing the Swanbrook livery. See next page.   *(V. Morgan).*

Above: This is the same Leyland 'Tiger' **A10 SBK**, as pictured on the previous page, after a repaint and refurbishment in November 2001. It was re-registered TIL 4527 in March 2002, and is seen as such, in the picture below.
Below: TIL 4527, previously *A10 SBK, E882 HFW, PS 2743, E510 RFU*, is seen on the bus wash at Ffoshelig. *(V. Morgan).*

Above: Former Bournemouth B.C. Leyland 'Leopard', **JLJ 109V**, with Plaxton 'Supreme IV Express' C53F coachwork, passed through Rhodri Evans hands in August 1999, in dealer capacity, but was re-purchased from Davies Coaches, Llanelli, in March 2001, in exchange for JIL 2433, a Volvo/Plaxton. Confusingly, it returned to Davies Coaches in January 2002.   *(V. Morgan).*

Above: Cherished registration **DSU 772** is seen once again on this Jonckheere 'Deauville 45' C53F bodied Volvo B10M-62, purchased in March 2001, from Clarkes, Lower Sydenham, London. New to Clarkes as *M326 KRY*, in April 1995, it's seen here at the M4 service area, Magor, on 19th May, 2001, working the company's first holiday tour to the Rhine Valley.   *(V.M).*

Above: In 2002, two identical Volvo B10M-61, Plaxton 'Supreme V' coaches were purchased from Hillman, Tredegar. First to arrive in February, was 57 seat **KXI 318**, *(YHR 702, TND 431X)*, which later passed to Davies Coaches, Llanelli. *(V. Morgan).*

Above: The second Volvo B10M-61, with Plaxton 'Supreme V' coachwork to arrive from Hillman (White Lion Cs), Tredegar in April 2002, was 53 seat, **HIL 2329**, *(BUA 161X, 9778 WA, VWX 363X)*, which returned to Hillman in April 2004. *(V. Morgan).*

Above: The first midi-coach purchased for the Ffoshelig fleet was this Toyota 'Coaster' HDB30R, with elegant Caetano 'Optimo II' C21F coachwork, **IIL 8521** *(J234 HVK)*, from Williams, Brecon, in July 2002. It retained Williams' livery, as it was almost identical to Ffoshelig's livery, and was sold locally to McKnight (Brook Cars) Laugharne, in May 2004.   *(V. Morgan)*.

Above: The company's first experience of Van-Hool coachwork, was this 'Alizee T8' body on Volvo B10M-61, **MUI 7389**, *(D345 KVE, DAZ 4300, D345 KVE)* from Kime, Folkingham, Lincolnshire, in November 2002. It's pictured here at Carmarthen on 13th October, 2003, with the town's famous landmark, County Hall, partially visible in the backdrop.   *(V. Morgan)*.

Plans to move the business from Ffoshelig Garage back to Rhodri Evans' original OC at Maes-y-Prior began in 2003, when a 12 month notice was issued to the depot owner, Des Jones. Work commenced at Maes-y-Prior in January 2004, to convert a farm building into a fully equipped workshop, allowing the complete operation to transfer in May 2004.

And by early 2004, a fleet of four limousines were added to the business, three Daimler DS420s, and a stretched Ford Granada built by the coachbuilders, Coleman Milne. Additionally, in September 2004, a non-PSV, eight seat Volkswagen Transporter minibus was acquired to operate feeder services for the coach holidays, besides other general uses.

FFOSHELIG
WEDDING CARS

Chauffeur Driven Daimler Limousines

Available for that
SPECIAL OCCASION

Weddings, Anniversaries, Birthdays, etc

01267 237584

Out of hours please telephone
07876 027926 - Emergencies only.

Ffoshelig Coaches,
Maes Y Prior, St. Peters,
Carmarthen, SA33 5DS

Produced and Printed by Withybush Printers Ltd. (01437) 769181

FFOSHELIG

Day Excursions
Short Breaks
& Holidays
2004

Local Joining Points
Uniformed Chauffeurs
Personal Service
Luxury Coaches
Easy Booking

01267 237584

Above: The 2004 excursions and holiday brochure, which included the intoduction of limousines into the fleet.

<u>Above:</u> Two of the company's Daimler DS420 limousines, **SIB 3294** and **DFM 393X**, pictured at a wedding. *(Rhodri Evans).*

<u>Above:</u> This attractive little Volkswagen Transporter, 7 seat personnel carrier, **CV02 LTA**, was purchased in September 2004, to operate feeder services for the company's coach holidays, besides being a general purpose vehicle. It had been converted into a personnel carrier by Cymric Conversions, when new to a private owner at Newport, Gwent, in July 2002. *(Rhodri Evans).*

Above: This immaculate Mercedes-Benz 'Vario' 0814D, with Autobus 'Nouvelle 2' C29F coachwork, **R91 GWO**, was new to Bebb's of Llantwit Fardre, Pontypridd, in January 1998, but was acquired via Miles, Stratton St Margaret, Wiltshire, in August 2004. It's seen here at the 'Maes-y-Prior' premises, and passed to Davies Coaches, Llanelli, in August 2005. *(Rhodri Evans).*

Above: Pride of the fleet in 2004 was this 1999, Kassbohrer-Setra S315GT-HD, **YSU 366** which arrived as *T255 GON*, in September 2004, from Silver Star, Caernarfon. It was re-registered before entering service in September 2004. *(Rhodri Evans).*

Above: Pictured here at the new depot, 'Maes-y-Prior', on 4th November, 2006, appropriately decorated with Christmas decorations, ready to depart on one of the 'Turkey and Tinsel' short breaks the following day, is **YSU 366**, *(T255 GON)*, a Kassbohrer-Setra 48 seat coach. This integrally built coach left the fleet in December 2009. *(V. Morgan).*

Above: **A475 TBX** *(YDE 679, A475 TBX)* was acquired from Jones of Login, Carmarthenshire, in August 2005. This view was taken on 4th June, 2006, when the coach was 22 years old. Despite its age, this Plaxton 'Paramount' bodied Volvo B10M-61, was absolutely immaculate, and was sold for further PSV use to a Lincolnshire operator in July 2015. *(V. Morgan).*

Above: To date, the only Scania operated was this L94IB4, **R6 HLC** *(R555 ELF, R6 HLC)*, with Irizar 'Inter Century' C57F coachwork, which remained in all-over white livery throughout its 14 month stay at Ffoshelig Coaches. *(V. Morgan).*

Above: Another splendid view of the Scania L94IB4, **R6 HLC**, taken at King Edward VII Avenue, Cardiff, on 11th March, 2006, when it was captured working an advertised excursion to Cardiff, for the WRU 'Six Nations' game between Wales and Italy. **R6 HLC** obtained its cherished registration mark when new to Lucketts Coaches, of Fareham, Hampshire. *(V. Morgan).*

Above: Former Jones of Login, DAF 400, with an Autobus 'Classique' PSV conversion, **L975 VDE**, was acquired via Davies Coaches, Llanelli, in August 2005, but operated on a private, seven seater licence, until sold in August 2006. *(V. Morgan).*

Above: The first vehicle to carry the cherished registration, **FF05 BUS**, was this Mercedes-Benz 'Vario' 0814D, with Plaxton 'Cheetah' C33F bodywork, which arrived new in September 2005, in all-over white livery. It was eventually repainted into normal fleet livery, and was re-registered CV55 MVM upon sale to Glyn Hicks of Mynyddcerrig, in July 2011. The cherished registration was retained by the company, and used on other company vehicles in due course. *(V. Morgan).*

Rhodri Evans
FFOSHELIG

Day Excursions, Short Breaks & Holidays 2006
☎ 01267 ~ 237584

The Highlights of Norway
9 days departing Thursday 21st September 2006

Thursday	Travel to Newcastle for the mid afternoon sailing from Newcastle on the DFDS overnight crossing to Kristiansand
Friday	Arrive in Kristiansand mid morning and travel along Norway's south coast to Oslo for a 3 night stay
Saturday	A guided morning sightseeing tour of Oslo, followed by an afternoon at leisure
Sunday	Morniing excursion to the Olympic Ski Jump at Holmenkellen and a relaxing afternoon in Oslo
Monday	Depart Oslo and enjoy a scenic day travelling across the Hardangervidda Mountain Road and the Hardangerfjord to the Oppheim Hotel for 3 nights
Tuesday	Full day optional "Norway in a Nutshell" excursion to include two scenic train journeys and a fjord cruise
Wednesday	A drive to the old village of Laerdaisoyri, and visit to the Wild Salmon Centre
Thursday	To Bergen with some free time to explore before we board the afternoon ferry to Newcastle
Friday	Arriving in Newcastle late afternoon we then head back to West Wales

Holiday Cost Includes
Return overnight ferries including inside cabins with private facilities
3 nights at the Scandic Hotel KSA Oslo
3 nights at the Oppheim Hotel, Oppheim
6 evening meals
6 full breakfasts
All coach Travel
Excursion as listed

Not included in Holiday Price
Meals while on board ferries
Admission Charges (unless stated)
Optional Norway in a Nutshell
Holiday Travel Insurance
Cabin upgrades

Cost of this holiday is £499.00 per person sharing a twin or double room.
Single room supplement £165.00
Holiday Travel Insurance £25.00
Norway in a Nutshell - to be confirmed

Opposite page: The front cover of Ffoshelig's '2006 Holidays, Short Breaks, and Day Excursions' brochure, together with just one example of their quality holidays.

An interesting development in June 2006, was the purchase of three vehicles from Frederick Elfed Lewis, of Whitland, who traded as Lewis Coaches, Whitland, together with the local service 227, from Carmarthen to Llanybri, and two schools services.

As stated on page 78, Elfed Lewis had acquired the 227 service, together with two school services, and three vehicles off Des Jones, the previous proprietor of Ffoshelig Coaches, when he retired and sold the business as three individual units in 1996. Ironically, this was 'Ffoshelig' work being re-united! That particular licence was registered as follows:-

PG 0006927/2   **Carmarthen (Bus Station)** to **Llanybri (Ger-y-Marbell)**. *Route No.227 via: Johnstown, Llangain and Llanstephan.   Normal stopping. Monday to Saturday, six return journeys daily.   Commencing 14/8/2006.*

And at the same time, the following new local service was registered:-

PG 0006927/1   **Carmarthen (Railway Stn)** to **Carmarthen Showground (Nantyci)**. *via: Lammas Street and Johnstown.   Route No.UCS1. To operate only when the 'United Counties Show' is held. Normal stopping.   Commencing 14/7/2006.*

Above: This is the only view I have of the former Lewis, Whitland, Mercedes-Benz 0814D, **YN53 VBO**, as it was acquired with accident damage, and only operated with Ffoshelig for a few days - in this livery. It was sent away for accident damage repairs to its Plaxton 'Beaver 2' bodywork, when an offer was made for it by a Tredegar operator, resulting in its inevitable sale, without returning to Carmarthen. *(V. Morgan).*

Above: Seen here leaving Carmarthen for Llanybri, on 16th August, 2006, is former Alpha Cs, Brighton, **SCD 693X**, a 1981 Leyland 'Leopard' PSU3F/4R with manual gearbox, and 11 metre Plaxton 'Supreme V' C53F coachwork. It had been acquired from Lewis, Whitland, two months earlier, for the 227 Llanybri service, with a genuine 232,263 km's on the clock. *(V. Morgan).*

Below: **SCD 693X**, is seen at the 'Plaxton Centenary' celebrations at Scarborough, 21st April, 2007. This immaculate coach was withdrawn after 30 years of service, and sold to a preservationist at Durham. Mileage 271,876 km's. *(P.R. Evans).*

Above: The third vehicle purchased from F.E. Lewis, Whitland, when he slimmed down his business in June 2006, was this Mercedes-Benz 'Vario' 0814D, **MX53 ZWD**, with Onyx C24F conversion. It will be noticed that since arrival of the Scania in 2005, the livery changed to white with red relief, but returned to pale cream with cardinal red relief in late 2006. **MX53 ZWD** passed to Isaac & Morgan (G & M Coaches), Lampeter, in October 2008, but returned to Lewis, Whitland, a year later! *(V. M.)*

Above: JUI 5931 *(K818 HUM)* was a Volvo B10M-60, with Van-Hool 'Alizee T8' C49FT coachwork, purchased from Isaac & Morgan (G & M Coaches), Lampeter, with the cherished registration in August 2006, and passed to the closely associated Davies Coaches, Llanelli, in July 2007. This vehicle was new to Wallace Arnold Tours, in March 1993, as *K818 HUM.* *(V.M.)*

Above: **N50 PDE** *(N21 EYB)* was a Volvo B10M-62, with Van-Hool 'Alizee T8' C53FT coachwork, acquired from Edwards, Tiers Cross, Pembrokeshire, in November 2006, and is seen here at Cardiff on the occasion of Wales v Ireland WRU game, 4th February, 2007, before it was re-registered with another cherished mark, VIL 9911 in April 2007, as shown below.
Below: **VIL 9911** was the 'new' cherished registration issued to *(N50 PDE, N21 EYB)*, seen above. *(Both, V. Morgan).*

Above: Integrally built Optare 'Solo' M990, B37F, **BU56 OOD** was purchased new in November 2006, specifically for the 227 service, and is seen arriving at Blue Street, (Carmarthen bus station), on its first journey of the day, 07.43 from Llanybri, via Llanstephan, Llangain, Johnstown, and Carmarthen bus station, terminating at Glangwili Hospital.
Below: **BU56 OOD** at Carmarthen on 20th December, 2006, before the extra lettering and red stripes were added. *(V. Morgan).*

Above: This Optare 'Solo' M850, **MX04 VLT**, was new to Stagecoach in April 2004, and returned to the Optare dealers at Cross Gates, Leeds, where it was used as a demonstrator. It was loaned to many operators, and worked for Rhodri Evans, Ffoshelig Coaches in November 2006, before sale to another welsh operator, Silcox, Pembroke Dock, in June 2007. *(V. M)*.

Above: Former Ministry of Defence, Leyland 'Tiger' *03 KJ 30*, with Plaxton 'Derwent II' body, arrived in February 2007, from EuroTaxis, Siston Common, Bristol, as *G828 XWS*, (without seats). It was fitted with 68 coach seats (3+2 seating) by Ffoshelig Coaches, and re-registered **YIL 8181** in April 2007. *(V. Morgan)*.

On 22nd March, 2007, P.R. Evans t/a Ffoshelig Coaches, applied for an increase of vehicle authorisation at the current operating centre, Maes-y-Prior, St Peters, Carmarthen.

The authorisation for 12 vehicles on licence PG 0006927/SI, was granted as applied for.

And as a result of successful tendering for a local authority supported service, the following local service was registered:-

PG 0006927/3 **Carmarthen (Bus Station)** to **Brecon**. *Route No. B10*
via: A40, Llandeilo and Llandovery.
To operate on Sundays & Bank Holiday Mondays from 27/5/07 to 9/9/07 only. Hail & Ride. *Commencing 27/5/2007.*

The above three trophies were won by Ffoshelig Coaches, at the 'All Wales Truck & Transport Show' held at Carmarthen Showground, Nantyci, Carmarthen, on Sunday 15th July, 2007. **Top left:** Best Coach Fleet, comprising of YSU 366 (Setra), SCD 693X, BU56 OOD and YIL 8181. **Top right:** Best Classic Coach: SCD 693X. **Bottom:** Best Coach: YSU 366.

Above: This Optare 'Tempo' X1260, 46 seat demonstrator **YJ07 EGD**, operated on loan to Ffoshelig Coaches, in July 2007.

Above: Personalised registration **RE57 FOS**, was issued to this Alexander-Dennis 'Javelin', with Plaxton 'Profile' C57F coachwork upon arrival in September 2007, and is still currently in the fleet. *(Rhodri Evans collection).*

Above: A second former Ministry of Defence, Leyland 'Tiger' with Plaxton 'Derwent II' bodywork, **G829 XWS**, was acquired from the closely associated business of Davies Coaches, Llanelli, in September 2007. Davies Coaches acquired it without seats, selling it on to Rhodri Evans, without operating it. Nevertheless, it was re-seated by Ffoshelig with 3+2 coach seating, to DP68F layout, and is pictured on layover, between duties, on 4th March, 2009. *(V. Morgan).*

Above: **PUI 3785** *(F512 LTT)*, was a Volvo B10M-60 with Van-Hool 'Alizee T8' C53F coachwork, acquired in October 2008, from Dawlish Coaches, Devon, and remained in all over white livery during its two year stay at Ffoshelig Coaches. *(V. Morgan).*

Above & Below: After seven years fitted to Rhodri Evans' company car, the cherished registration **V2 FOS**, was transferred to this integrally built Kassbohrer–Setra 'S315GT-HD' 53 seater, upon arrival in October 2008, from Clarkes of Lower Sydenham, London. Previously registered *Y586 TOV*, it was new to Clarkes in April 2001, and returned to its original registration in October 2013, before sale to 'Cavern City Coaches', Liverpool. This coach was Rhodri's pride and joy, and is photographed at the depot on 13th May, 2009. Incidentally, there was nothing wrong with the LED destination display - that is exactly how the camera picks up LED illuminated destination displays. *(V. Morgan).*

<u>Above:</u> Former Western Scottish (V334), **M734 BSJ**, was acquired in November 2008, from Ridgeways of Port Talbot. This Volvo B6-50 with Alexander 'Dash' B40F bodywork, looked superb in the Ffoshelig livery, but it certainly did not stay very long, it was withdrawn within 9 months and sold for scrap 3 months later. *(V. Morgan).*

The bus pictured above, M734 BSJ, was purchased in November 2008, for a commercially operated local service, which was registered as follows:-

PG 0006927/4 **Carmarthen (Bus Station)** to **Bancyfelin.**   *Route No.219*
via: Johnstown.
One journey only, Mon to Sat. inc. Good Friday. No other Bank Holidays.
Hail & Ride.   Commencing 5/1/2009.
This service was cancelled from 19/4/2009.

And in early 2009, successful local authority tendering brought about the registration of two more local services:-

PG 0006927/5 **Carmarthen (Bus Station)** to **Carmarthen (Bus Station)** *Route No.207*
via: Brynmeurig, Login Road, and Llangunnor (circular).
One evening journey only, Monday to Saturday including Good Friday.
Hail & Ride.   Commencing 20/4/2009.

PG 0006927/6 **Carmarthen (Bus Stn)** to **Carmarthen (Russell Terr.)** *Route No.206*
via: Brewery Road.
One evening journey only, Monday to Saturday including Good Friday.
Hail & Ride.   Commencing 20/4/2009.

Later that year, Terry Treharne, the former MD of West Wales Motors Ltd, Tycroes, joined the staff of Ffoshelig, and influenced Rhodri Evans to challenge First Cymru Buses on their daily Carmarthen to Pendine service. Rhodri ultimately agreed, and the service was registered as below:-

PG 0006927/7 **Carmarthen (Railway Station)** to **Pendine (Church)**. *Route No.222*
via: Carmarthen bus station, Johnstown, St Clears and Laugharne.
Monday to Saturday including Good Friday. No other Bank Holidays.
Normal stops. Hail & Ride. Commencing 23/11/2009.

First Cymru Buses were not prepared to accept a challenge on this route, and immediately stood down, surrendering their licence, which enabled Ffoshelig Coaches to claim the financial support available for this service, as previously authorised to First Cymru Buses.

On 7th December, 2009, licences PG 0006927/5 and PG 0006927/6 were surrendered, and simultaneously, the following tendered local services were registered:-

PG 0006927/8 **Carmarthen (Bus Station)** to **Parc Dewi Sant**. *Route No.226*
via: Trinity College, Parc Dewi Sant, Johnstown, Llanstephan Road and Davies' Estate.
Monday to Friday only, not Bank Holidays, except Good Fridays.
Hail & Ride. Commencing 7/12/2009.

PG 0006927/9 **Brechfa** to **Carmarthen (Bus Station)**. *Route No.282*
via: Nantgaredig Square, Capel Dewi and Llangunnor.
Monday to Saturday, not Bank Holidays, except Good Fridays.
Hail & Ride. Commencing 7/12/2009.

PG 0006927/10 **Carmarthen (Bus Station)** to **Carmarthen (Bus Station)**.
'Dial-A-Ride' service. Flexible registration, Route Nos. B11, B12, B13
Monday to Saturday, not Bank Holidays, except Good Fridays.
Commencing 7/12/2009.

The following tendered local service was registered a year later:-

PG 0006927/11 **Carmarthen (Railway Station)** to **Brechfa**. *Route No. 282*
via: Llangunnor, Capel Dewi and Nantgaredig Square.
Monday to Saturday, not Bank Holidays except Good Fridays.
Hail & Ride. Commencing 20/12/2010.

By this point in time, Rhodri Evans' family had already retired from the farm at Maes-y-Prior, and were renting the farmland to neighbouring farms, rendering all farm outbuildings redundant. Setting up a subsidiary business, Rhodri was granted planning permission to convert these redundant buildings into 'Holiday Barns'. Renovation commenced in October

2011, and work on this collection of beautifully restored traditional 'Welsh Barns', with the luxuries of home, was completed in early 2013, and were open for business under the title of **'Best Barns in Wales'**, in time for Easter 2013.   www.thebestbarnsinwales.co.uk

Above: This is a general view of the traditional 'Welsh Barns' at Maes-y-Prior, situated in beautiful countryside within a half mile of the A40 trunk road, between Carmarthen and St Clears, in south-west Wales.

Above: This is a view of 'The Smithy', a luxurious 2 berth accomodation.

These two views show the high standards accomplished in the lounge and kitchen area's of these 'Welsh Barns'.

Above: Pictured at Carmarthen Leisure Centre on 13th May, 2009, is this Polish built Autosan 'Eagle' A1012T, C68F (3+2) integral coach, re-registered with cherished mark, **DS56 FOS**, before entering service April 2009. It was new to Goulden, Welwyn Garden City, Hertfordshire, in September 2006, as *BX56 XAL*, and acquired by Ffoshelig in February 2009.   *(Both views, V. Morgan).*
Below: The Autosan, at Morrison's store, Carmarthen, shortly before its sale to Morris Travel, Carmarthen, as BX56 XAL.

Above: Pictured at Cambrian Place, Carmarthen, on 7th April, 2010, in all-over white livery, as received, is **WD03 WVW**, a Volvo B7R-63, with Jonckheere 'Modulo' C53F coachwork. This was new in May 2003, to O'Shea, Ballyheigue, Co. Kerry, Republic of Ireland, as 03-KY-2698, and arrived here in August 2009, from Hilton, Newton-le-Willows, where it received this UK registration.
Below: Looking really superb, **WD03 WVW**, was captured here on 9th July, 2010, soon after receiving fleet livery. *(V. Morgan).*

Above: **B6 PRE**, was the personalised registration mark applied to Volvo B7R-63, *WD03 WVW*, pictured opposite, and was retained by Ffoshelig upon sale to Evans, Steynton, Milford Haven, in August 2017, returning to *WD03 WVW*, once again. *(V. M)*.

Above: Rhodri Evans, acquired **R705 MNU,** *(previously WYM 675, originally R705 MNU)* a Volvo B10M-62, with Plaxton 'Premiere 320' coachwork, from Ken Hopkins, Tonna, West Glam, in July 2009, and immediately sent it away for painting into fleet livery. It returned a month later, minus vynals, when Elfed Lewis (Lewis Coaches) Whitland, badgered Rhodri into selling it. Without being operated, it passed to Lewis in August 2009, who operated it in Ffoshelig's livery, as seen on 9th November, 2009. *(V.M)*.

Above: This integrally built Optare 'Versa' V1100, with B38F layout, **YJ59 NMZ**, was purchased initially for the Carmarthen to Pendine, 222 service, and arrived new in November 2009. It was captured here on 11th February, 2010, leaving Carmarthen bus station for its final destination, Carmarthen Railway Station, situated ¼ mile away from the bus station, across the river Towy.

Below: Is a nearside view of the Optare 'Versa', **YJ59 NMZ**, leaving Carmarthen bus station for Pentywyn, the welsh name for Pendine, expertly driven by the proprietor, Rhodri Evans. After the Pendine service was withdrawn on 19th February, 2011, this vehicle became the mainstay of the Carmarthen – Llanybri service, until its eventual sale in July 2013.   *(Both views, V. Morgan).*

Above: 21 seat Optare 'Solo' M710SE, **YJ59 NNY**, arrived new in January 2010, to operate the newly acquired local authority supported, Carmarthen town 'Dial-a-Ride' services, which are centred upon the bus station. The contract specified a white liveried vehicle, but it was accidentally painted into fleet livery by Optare, and accepted by the authority. It was captured on 22nd September, 2010, leaving the bus station on the B12 across town service, between Glynderi, and Morrison's Store, Pensarn.   *(V. Morgan).*

Above: Former London General, LDP1, **P501 RYM**, was purchased in March 2010, as a relief vehicle for the Pendine service. Its engine had to be replaced soon after purchase, and in February 2011, this bus passed to Richards Bros, Cardigan. *(V. Morgan).*

Rhodri Evans-Ffoshelig Coaches

Don't hire any old bus !
Ffoshelig Coaches have a fleet of modern coaches from 24 to 67 seats available for all occasions.

We also operate local bus services from Carmarthen to Llanstephan, Llanybri, St Clears, Laugharne and Pendine.
For a full list visit our website.

Call for a free brochure or quotation

Ffoshelig Coaches, Maes y Prior, St Peters, Carmarthen, SA33 5DS
01267 237584

Or visit our Website at
www.ffoshelig.co.uk

Above: The third vehicle in the fleet to carry the cherished registration **DSU 772**, was this Volvo B10M-62, with Van-Hool 'Alizee T9' C49FT coachwork, acquired from Richmond, of Barley, Hertfordshire, in August 2010, as *EJ52 UYS*, (originally *649 ETF*). It was captured here on 21st September, 2011, still in Richmond's livery, but received fleet livery soon afterwards.   *(V. Morgan).*

Below: **DSU 772** *(EJ52 UYS, 649 ETF)* in fleet livery. It returned to EJ52 UYS in December 2017, before sale to an Irish operator.

Above: EJ52 UYS, previously *DSU 772, EJ52 UYS, 649ETF*, seen on the preceeding page, was photographed in pouring rain at the depot, on the day it departed in March 2018, for its new home with Lixnaw Coaches, at Lixnaw, County Kerry, in the Republic of Ireland. It received the registration number 02-KY-10223, on arrival at Lixnaw Coaches. *(Rhodri Evans).*

Above: N711 AHP was a Plaxton 'Premiere 350' bodied Volvo B10M-62, which had been leased to Bus Eireann (VP9) in the Republic of Ireland when new in December 1995, as *95-D-41599*. It returned to England in 1998, where it was dealer re-registered **N711 AHP** in 1999, and passed to Llynfi Coaches, Maesteg, Mid-Glamorgan. Ffoshelig Coaches acquired it from Llynfi in September 2010, already converted to C70F layout (3+2 seating), adding the vinyl's to its yellow 'school bus' livery. *(V. Morgan).*

<u>Above:</u> A 'new' personalised registration mark **DS11 FOS**, was acquired and issued to this Mercedes-Benz 'Vario' 0816D, when it arrived brand new in April 2011. The coachwork built by Plaxton, was branded as the 'Cheetah', built to C33F layout, with air conditioning (the pod on its roof). It is photographed here at Trafalgar Square, London. *(Rhodri Evans' collection).*

Surprisingly, the obligatory notice was given on 29th December, 2010, to terminate the road service licence for the 222 Carmarthen to Pendine service. This was due to a huge reduction in concessionary fare reimbursement from the Welsh Assembly, and subsidies from the local authority, Carmarthenshire C.C.

The 222 service was withdrawn as from 19th February, 2011, and an arrangement was drawn up with Taf-Valley Coaches (Bysiau Cwm-Taf), Whitland, for them to take over the service on licence number, PG 0007573/14, as from 21st February, 2011.

On the brighter side, eight months later in October 2011, Rhodri Evans absorbed the goodwill and remaining licences of Frederick Elfed Lewis' business at Whitland. No vehicles or premises were acquired in the transaction, but Elfed accepted a part time vocation at Ffoshelig Coaches, with the official transfer of Lewis' business taking place on 1st November, 2011.

At the same time, Rhodri Evans' associate, Kenneth Alun Davies, (Davies Coaches, Llanelli), officially withdrew his additional operating centre at Maes-y-Prior, St Peters, Carmarthen, replacing it with a new operating centre at Unit 12, Crofty Industrial Estate, Penclawdd, Swansea, SA4 3RS, having taken over the former 'Veolia Transport Cymru' depot, at Crofty Industrial Estate, Penclawdd.

Shortly afterwards came the unwelcome news of a substantial reduction in the 'Bus Service Operator Grant' (fuel duty rebate) paid by central government. From 1st April, 2012, the BSOG was reduced by 25%, coupled to a 27% reduction in Local Transport Service Grants.

These financial cuts were a tremendous blow to struggling rural bus operators, which inevitably led Rhodri to terminate his licence for the 227 Carmarthen to Llanybri service, (PG 0006927/2), as from 10th February, 2013. At the same time, negotiations took place with the local authority, Carmarthenshire C.C., resulting in some extra financial support, in order for the service to continue, which then had to be re-registered as shown below:-

   PG 0006927/12   **Carmarthen (Bus Stn)** to **Llanybri (Ger-y-Marbell)**. *Route No.227*
                           via: Llangain and Llanstephan.
                           Monday to Saturday, including Good Fridays, except Bank Holidays.
                                         Hail & Ride. Commencing 10/2/2013.

Nevertheless, the 227 service was terminated again seven months later on Saturday, 13th September, 2013, and passed to Morris Travel, Carmarthen, who bought Ffoshelig's Optare 'Solo' registered MP51 BUZ, to run the service. At the same time, one driver transferred to Morris Travel with the service.

Above: The current business card for Ffoshelig Coaches.

INCORPORATION

Taking into consideration the financial cuts experienced in the preceding two years, Rhodri decided it was time to register the business as a private limited company, in order to safeguard himself from heavy losses in the event of business failure.

Ffoshelig Coaches Ltd, was incorporated on 11th March, 2013, as company number 08439005. The Managing Director is recorded as Phillip Rhodri Evans, and the Secretary, Debbie Diana Evans, Rhodri Evans' wife.

However, the application to modify the operator licence accordingly, was not submitted until 13th February, 2014, and was granted on 27th March, 2014, with a new operator number due to change of entity, as follows:-

PG 1127013/SI: Ffoshelig Coaches Ltd., Maes-y-Prior, St Peters, Carmarthen, SA33 5DS.

Directors: Phillip Rhodri Evans, and Debbie Diana Evans.

Transport Manager: Phillip Rhodri Evans.

Authorisation: 14 vehicles.

Following the change of entity above, all road service licences held had to be exchanged, in order to carry the new operator number. Therefore, licences PG 0006927/8, PG 0006927/9 and PG 0006927/10 were all cancelled from 8th June, 2014, and superseded the following day by:-

PG 1127013/1 **Carmarthen (Bus Station)** to **Parc Dewi Sant.** *Route No.226*
via: Morfa Lane, Glannant Road, and College Road.
Monday to Friday, not Bank Holidays, except Good Fridays.
One journey in each direction.   Hail & Ride.   Commencing 9/6/2014.

PG 1127013/2 **Brechfa** to **Carmarthen (Bus Station).** *Route No.282*
via: Felingwm Uchaf, Nantgaredig and Capel Dewi.
Monday to Saturday, not Bank Holidays, except Good Fridays.
One journey in each direction.   Hail & Ride.   Commencing 9/6/2014.

PG 1127013/4 **Carmarthen (Bus Station)** to **Carmarthen (Bus Station)** *Route No.B11*
via: Llanllwch, Parc-y Ffordd, and Cilddewi Park.
Monday to Saturday, not Bank Holidays, except Good Fridays.
Hail & Ride.   Commencing 9/6/2014.

PG 1127013/5 **Carmarthen (Bus Station)** to **Pensarn (Morrison Store)** *Route No.B12*
via: Tanerdi, Glynderi and Llwyn Meredydd.
Monday to Saturday, not Bank Holidays, except Good Fridays.
Hail & Ride.   Commencing 9/6/2014.

PG 1127013/6 **Carmarthen (Bus Station)** to **Pensarn (Morrison Store)** *Route No.B13*
via: Cwmffrwd, Tregynnwr, and Penymorfa.
Monday to Saturday, not Bank Holidays, except Good Fridays.
Hail & Ride. Commencing 9/6/2014.

PG 1127013/7 **Carmarthen (Bus Station)** to **Carmarthen (Bus Station)**.
Named Carmarthen Dial a Ride. Service type – Flexible Registrations.
Monday to Saturday, Not Bank Holidays, except Good Fridays.
Hail & Ride. Commencing 9/6/2014.

PG 1127013/8 **Four Roads (Kidwelly)** to **Carmarthen (Q E High School)**. *No.QEH1*
via: Mynydd-y-Garreg, and Kidwelly.
Monday to Friday, Schooldays only.
Schools service.   Commencing 8/7/2014.

It will be noticed that PG 1127013/3 was a number not used.

Due to fierce competition in the area, the company's last advertised Holiday Tour operated to Prestatyn, North Wales, on 10th November, 2014. It was a 'Turkey & Tinsel' short break, at the end of the 2014 holiday season, which had 35 passengers on board.

Above: In August 2011, a pair of consecutively registered, immaculate, Dennis Javelins, **X847/8 XDE**, fitted with Plaxton 'Premiere 320' C70F coachwork (3+2 seating), arrived from Jones Motors, Login, Carmarthenshire, where they were new in February 2001. Pictured on 21st September, 2011, is **X847 XDE**, numerically first of the pair, which was looking splendid at almost 11 years old. *(V. Morgan).*

Above: The second Plaxton 'Premiere 320' C70F bodied coach from the pair of Dennis Javelins acquired from Jones, Login, in August 2011, was **X848 XDE**, which was captured here at Parc-y-Scarlets on 24th September, 2011. Both stablemates continued to be united, as the pair passed to Talley-Ho Coaches, of Kingsbridge, Devon in August 2016. *(V. Morgan).*

Above: This little Optare 'Solo' M850, 27 seat bus, **MP51 BUZ**, was one of two vehicles bought from John Morrow, Glasgow, in April 2012. This 'BUZ' was sold in October 2013, with the 227 service, to Morris Travel, Carmarthen. The other vehicle acquired from John Morrow, was a Mercedes-Benz 'Vario' 0814D, which is pictured on page 173. *(V. Morgan).*

Above: SF55 PSY was another Mercedes-Benz 'Vario' 0814D, which had Plaxton 'Beaver II' bodywork built to DP29FL layout, with a wheelchair lift, and is seen working the Carmarthen 'Dial-a-Ride' service, B13, on 25th November, 2013. *(V. Morgan).*

Above: Cherished registration **FF05 BUS** was reused on this Berkhof' Axial 50' bodied DAF SB4000, when it arrived from Golden Tours, Victoria, London, in October 2013. It returned to YJ08 ECX in January 2016, before sale to Bennetts, of Stafford.

Above: Another reused cherished registration mark, **V2 FOS**, appeared on this 10 metre Volvo B7R, with Sunsundegui 'Sideral' C44F coachwork, after arrival in July 2014. Previously registered *FN09 AOA*, it was new to Priory City of Lincoln Academy, in May 2009, and is currently still operating with Ffoshelig Coaches in 2021. *(Rhodri Evans collection).*

Above: Seen here working the Carmarthen 'Dial-a-Ride' service is **YJ55 YGX**, a 23 seat Optare 'Solo' M850SL, which came from Compass, Worthing, in September 2014. It was sold in December 2018, when all Ffoshelig's local services ceased. *(V.M)*.

Above & Below: Previously owned by Ffoshelig as *DSU 772*, this Volvo B10M-62 was re-acquired from Davies Coaches, Llanelli, in February 2015, bearing the registration **JIL 7657**. That cherished registration was returned to Davies Coaches before it entered service with Ffoshelig, and reverted to its original registration mark, **M326 KRY**. In August 2016 however, it was re-registered XUD 367 – see opposite. *(V. Morgan).*

Above: The cherished registration mark, **XUD 367**, previously owned by Silcox Coaches, was purchased at an auction held after Silcox's demise in 2016, and fitted to the Jonckheere bodied Volvo B10M-62, *M326 KRY*, which is pictured opposite. When this coach passed to Evans, Steynton, in April 2018, the registration mark left with it, but when the coach later passed to Mike Hayward, the Carmarthen operator/dealer, the registration **XUD 367** was sold back to Ffoshelig Coaches. *(V. Morgan).*

Above: Former Ministry of Defence *NU07 YGH*, a Volvo B7R, Plaxton 'Profile' arrived via Snaith, Otterburn, Northumberland, in August 2015, as *YV07 PVJ*, but immediately received cherished registration **DS56 FOS** - which was removed upon sale.

Above: From the point of inception in 2013, Ffoshelig's coaches were bilingually sign written. Welsh being management's first language was used on the near side, and English on the off-side, as displayed by former Ministry of Defence, Plaxton 'Profile' bodied, Volvo B7R, **DS56 FOS** *(YV07 PVJ, NU07 YGH)*. The lettering is Cardinal Red with black shadowing, on the standard fleet livery of Pale Cream coachwork. 'Teithiau Moethus' translated to English is of course – Luxury Travel.

Above: The first 'new' vehicle to appear in the fleet for five years, was **RE65 FOS**, a superb integrally built Mercedes-Benz 'Tourismo' 55 seat coach, which arrived in January 2016. This view was taken on 6th June, 2016. *(V. Morgan).*

Above: Another view of the Mercedes-Benz 'Tourismo', with personalised registration mark **RE65 FOS**, showing the English version of branding, 'Ffoshelig Luxury Travel'. This coach was still owned at the time of going to press. *(Rhodri Evans).*

Above: This Mercedes-Benz 'Tourismo M' demonstrator, **BL16 FYV**, operated on loan from Evobus (dealer) Coventry in August 2016, and is seen here working a short break to St Ives, for 'Leisuretime', on 16th August, 2016. *(Rhodri Evans).*

Above: **FF05 BUS** is the Kassbohrer-Setra S416GT-HD integral *(BV55 FPN)* mentioned in the caption of the picture opposite. It was acquired from Lodge, of High Easter, Essex, in September 2016, and was new to Kings Ferry Coaches, of Gillingham, Kent, in February 2006. It was photographed at Cardiff, still in Lodge's livery, shortly before it received fleet livery.

Above: Looking really outstanding in Ffoshelig's pale cream livery, with cardinal red lettering, is the same Kassbohrer-Setra, S416GT-HD, with its cherished registration, **FF05 BUS**, previously *(BV55 FPN, 46 AEW, originally BV55 FPN).*

(Rhodri Evans).

Above: In September 2016, the company had this Auwarter-Neoplan N2216/3SHDC demonstrator, **OU16 EWW**, on loan from the dealers MAN, of Trafford Park, and is pictured here on the yard, alongside newly acquired Kassbohrer-Setra, BV55 FPN. This view was taken on 16th September, 2016, as the coach was ready to depart for Bruges, Belgium. *(Rhodri Evans).*

Above: Ffoshelig Coaches complimentary slip.

With effect from 2/9/2016, the local service registered under PG 1127013/8, Four Roads, (Kidwelly) to Carmarthen (Queen Elizabeth High School), was cancelled.

Above: This Mercedes-Benz 'Vario' 0814D, **YN54 DDV**, with Plaxton 'Cheetah' C33F coachwork, was acquired in September 2017, from Apple Travel, Slough, Bucks, and remained in all-over white livery throughout its eleven month stay at Ffoshelig. This view was taken at the depot on 9th Aug., 2018, with Kassbohrer-Setra, FF05 BUS, visible in the backdrop. *(Rhodri Evans)*.

Above: A splendid near side view of the same Mercedes-Benz 'Vario' **YN54 DDV**, displays clearly the extended overhang with the Plaxton 'Cheetah' coachwork. Both views were taken on 9th August, 2018 – the day it left Ffoshelig Coaches, to join a new local operator, Richard Spiller (2 Impress Travel), at nearby St Clears. *(Rhodri Evans)*.

Above: When this publication was being compiled in early 2021, the company were beginning to celebrate their centenary, and to celebrate the occasion, most of the vehicles in the fleet were treated to very impressive bilingual centenary branding.
Pictured here, displaying the centenary branding in March 2021, is VDL (Bova) Futura, C54FT, issued with a pre-used personalised registration mark, **B6 PRE**.
This coach was purchased from Williams Coaches, Brecon, Powys, in December 2017, a company with similar livery, having previously been registered, *WA11 HXL*.
(Rhodri Evans).

Right: An excellent rear end shot of the VDL (Bova) Futura, **B6 PRE**, before it was treated with the centenary branding.
(Rhodri Evans).

Above: Latest addition to the 'personalised registration' list is **B10 PRE**, previously *YN58 CFX*. This Dennis 'Javelin' with Plaxton 'Profile' C70F coachwork, was re-registered upon arrival from Swan's Travel, Chadderton, Oldham, in September 2018. *(Rhodri Evans).*

Above: The fourth Plaxton 'Profile' in the fleet was re-registered upon arrival in October 2018, with a 'recycled' cherished registration, **DSU 772**. Previously registered *YN60 FMG*, this Dennis 'Javelin' was new in November 2010, to Roy McCarthy Coaches, Macclesfield, Cheshire, as a 70 seater, and retains the same seating arrangement. *(Rhodri Evans).*

On 11th November, 2018, the company operated their last local services. A combination of issues were responsible for the withdrawal of these services, but the main issue was a reduction in Concessionary Fare reimbursement. Besides, there was no incentive after financial cuts were made to Local Service Grants in 2012, coupled with the fact that it became difficult to cover shifts when the regular driver was off. Additionally, it had become impossible to recruit part time drivers for local service work, after the two regular relief drivers had retired.

The final six local services operated, are listed below:-

PG 1127013/1   Carmarthen (Bus Station) to Parc Dewi Sant.   *Route No.226*

PG 1127013/2   Brechfa to Carmarthen (Bus Station).   *Route No.282*

PG 1127013/4 to 7   Carmarthen 'Dial-a-Ride' flexible registrations, and *B11, B12, B13*

Above: Another demonstration vehicle landed at Ffoshelig Coaches' premises shortly before Christmas 2018. On this occasion, it was an integrally built Mercedes-Benz 'Tourismo M3', with C57FT coachwork, registered **BF67 WLK**, on loan from dealers, Evo-Bus (UK) Ltd. of Coventry. This coach, which was new in February 2018, was well used and evaluated by the company, and was photographed working a private hire assignment to Cadbury World, at Linden Road, Birmingham, on 22nd December, 2018. The following week, it was used for another private charter, to Disneyland, Paris, before it eventually returned to its owners in January 2019.   *(Rhodri Evans).*

Above: The fifth vehicle acquired with Plaxton 'Profile' coachwork was another 'Javelin' chassis, but now built by Alexander-Dennis. **YN59 BMO** was the second 'Javelin' acquired from Roy McCarthy Coaches, Macclesfield, in May 2019. *(P.R. Evans)*.

Above: K51 TER is a Volvo B10M-60 with Van-Hool 'Alizee T8' C50FT coachwork, and at 28 years old, is currently the oldest vehicle in the fleet. It was acquired from Kenzies Coaches, Shepreth, Cambs, in September 2019, and retains the Kenzies livery, due to the unprecedented times of 'Covid 19' lockdown. *(Rhodri Evans)*.

Above: This little expedition, to the 'Black Mountain', near Brynamman, Carmarthenshire, on 11th March, 2020, was the last private hire worked by **K51 TER**, before the famous Coronavirus lockdown of 2020. The Black Mountain range, forms part of the Brecon Beacons National Park, which extends from Llandeilo in the west, to Abergavenny in the east. *(Rhodri Evans).*

Above: Former Ministry of Defence Dennis 'Javelin', with Plaxton 'Prima' C55F body, **MIG 1727**, was purchased off Hayward, dealer/operator, Carmarthen, in November 2019, but was returned 11 months later, in exchange for a 'Setra'. *(Rhodri Evans).*

Above: A splendid rear end shot of the former Ministry of Defence Dennis 'Javelin', **MIG 1727**, shows how much free advertising space the associated business obtained on the coaches. This coach was originally registered *MU51 FDJ* with the M o D, beginning civilian life in January 2014, re-registered *CP51 ZBE*, changing to **MIG 1727** in March 2014. *(Rhodri Evans).*

The next major issue in the history of Ffoshelig Coaches, was an issue which affected *every* passenger vehicle operator nationwide.

It was the unprecedented times of 'National Lockdown', brought about by the Covid-19 pandemic, which resulted in Ffoshelig's school contract vehicles operating their last school runs on 20th March, 2020, until the new academic year started in September 2020, with the exception of two vehicles from 29th June to 17th July, when schools reopened on a complex basis for some classes.

Additionally, between March and May 2020, several journeys were made to Heathrow Airport, conveying International Students from the university in Carmarthen, to catch flights back home to their relevant countries.

Apart from that, some rail replacement work was undertaken between March and September 2020, and when the lockdown rules were somewhat relaxed, a few private hires operated from August to October.

Therefore, it was a welcome relief to everyone involved, to see schools reopen at the beginning of the academic year in September 2020, in order to receive some revenue.

However, a second lockdown was enforced, and the last private hire to operate before the second lockdown at the end of October 2020, was a four day tour centred upon Mid-Wales, and based at Aberystwyth from 17th October, to 20th October, 2020.

School contracts however, remained operational during the second lockdown, but finished early for Christmas on 11th December, 2020, and did not return until 15th March, 2021. They continued uninterrupted from 15th March, until the end of term in July, but the private hire section of the business did not restart until 24th May, 2021.

Above: This spectacular view was taken in the Elan Valley, near Rhyader, Mid-Wales, on Monday 19th October, 2020, when Ffoshelig Coaches operated the last day of a 4 day tour, based at Aberystwyth. It was the last private hire operated before the second lockdown was enforced in October 2020. The coach operating this tour, **FF05 BUS**, a Kassbohrer-Setra, is just visible on the left hand side of this view. The Elan Valley reservoirs, situated at the edge of the Cambrian Mountains, are a chain of man-made lakes created between 1893-6, by damming the Elan and Claerwen rivers, and were built by Birmingham Corporation Water Department, to provide drinking water for Birmingham. *(Rhodri Evans).*

Above: Rhodri Evans, the MD of Ffoshelig Coaches has a penchant for the Setra marque, and purchased this S315GT-HD, **BU51 FXF**, from Mike Hayward, Carmarthen, during the extraordinary times of National Lockdown in October 2020. It's pictured **Below** after its re-registration to **XUD 367**, and a repaint into fleet livery, with branding added to celebrate Ffoshelig's centenary. Ffoshelig Coaches are currently the longest serving privately owned passenger vehicle operator in South Wales.

Above: A splendid near side view of the 49 seat Kassbohrer-Setra S315GT-HD, **XUD 367**, displaying the intricate artwork of the branding, for the company's centenary. Welsh being the operator's first language, is used on the near side, English on the off side. The English translation of "Canmlwyddiant FFOSHELIG Mynd yn Hir Mynd yn Gyf " is "Going Long, Going Strong FFOSHELIG Centenary".   *(Rhodri Evans).*

Above: The VDL 'Futura', **B6 PRE**, was already lettered "Teithiau Moethus FFOSHELIG" – "FFOSHELIG Luxury Travel" when the centenary branding was introduced. The 100 year laural leaf emblem was simply added to that.   *(Rhodri Evans).*

Above: Ffoshelig Coaches' Leyland 'Leopard', **SCD 693X** attended the Plaxton Coachworks centenary celebrations at Scarborough on 21st April, 2007, and is seen here on Foreshore Road, Scarborough, during the cavelcade. *(Rhodri Evans)*.

Above: Ffoshelig Coaches' depot at Maes-y-Prior, St Peters, Carmarthen, taken during lockdown in October 2020, when all the fleet except one, were visible. Both workshops are in the foreground, and the depot office is situated in the top left hand corner. *(Daniel James).*

This facinating story of Ffoshelig Coaches, is a succinct history of the business to date, and was compiled to complement the company's centenary celebrations.

Ffoshelig Coaches are currently the longest serving privately owned passenger vehicle operator in South Wales, and I would like to wish the current directors of Ffoshelig Coaches, Rhodri and Debbie Evans, their continued success, and hopefully another 100 years of dependable first class service.

Above: The Ffoshelig Coaches' centenery branding, was applied to all coaches in January 2021. The branding is bilingual, with the English version, applied to off-side panels, whilst the Welsh version (below) was applied to the near-side panels. All lettering is Cardinal Red, with Black shadowing.

Above: The Welsh version of Ffoshelig Coaches' centenery branding, which was applied to the near-side of all coaches in January 2021.

D. JONES (FFOSHELIG COACHES) VEHICLE DETAILS

Reg. No	Chassis make & type	Chassis number	Body make & type	Seating	Date New	Remarks / Additional Information Previous Owner	Date Acquired	Date Withdrawn
BX 1277	Vulcan 20 hp lorry u/w under 2 ton		Lorry with van body		5/1920	Green livery	12/5/1920	?
	Daimler			B20	1921	Named 'Newchurch Pride'	1921	?
BX 7410	Guy BA	5364		B20F	12/1926	New	12/1926	1932
TH 1209	Morris Commercial		Tipper lorry	B20F	10/1930	New	10/1930	?
TX 8740	GMC T30	303300		B20-	1/1930	New to G. Davies, Resolven, Glam. Ex T. Davies, 'Osborne Services'. Neath.	4/1931	5/1941
TH 2283	Morris Commercial		Tipper lorry		2/1932	New	2/1932	?
TH 2510	Bedford WHB	100044	Duple	C14-	5/1932	New	5/1932	5/1941
TH 9099	Bedford WTB u/w 3t 18cwt 2qr	111218	Thomas & Thomas	C25F	7/1937	New	7/1937	11/1952
BTH 777	Bedford OWB u/w 3t 6cwt	9339	Duple	B32F to B28F	10/1942	New	10/1942	11/1950
CBX 160	Bedford		Lorry		12/1943	New	12/1943	?
CTH 555	Bedford OYD		Lorry		10/1946	New	10/1946	?
TH 4455	Fordson BB n/c u/w 2t 17cwt	6359		20	6/1934	New to Ivor Williams, Trelech. Carmarthenshire. Ex J.R. Davies. Talog, Carmarthenshire.	3/1947	1947
SX 5044	Bedford WTB 28hp	17919	Duple	C26F	5/1939	Ex Campbell Bros. Whitburn, West Lothian.	5/1947	1951
ACJ 968	Bedford WTB	111745		C26F	1/1938	Ex Sargeants Motors. Kington, Herefordshire.	6/1947	1950
DTH 999	Bedford OB u/w 3t 12cwt	73901	Duple 'Vista'	C29F	4/1948	New	4/1948	8/1959

Reg	Chassis	Serial	Body	Seats	New	History	Acquired	Disposed
EBX 666	Bedford OB	61072	Thomas & Thomas	C29F	7/1948	New	lic. 8/1948	8/1959
DWN 256	Bedford OWB	10566	Duple (Utility)	B32F	12/1942	Ex United Welsh Services, Swansea (660). via Thomas & Jones (Precelly Motors), Efail Wen, Clynderwen, Pembrokeshire.	12/1948	11/1950
ETH 888	Bedford OB u/w 3t 12cwt	102572	Mulliner	B31F	4/1949	New	lic. 5/1949	9/1957
FDE 623	Bedford OWB	13856	Duple (Utility)	B32F to B30F	5/1943	Ex Richards Bros, Moylegrove, Pembs. via Thomas & Jones (Precelly Motors), Efail Wen, Clynderwen, Pembs.	8/1951	12/1955
LPU 620	Bedford OB u/w 3t 3cwt	69986	Beadle	B30F	2/1948	Ex Eastern National O.C. (3930). via United Counties O.C. (112). and D.J. Morrison. Tenby, Pembrokeshire (26).	12/1955	4/1965
DBD 936	Bedford OB	68033	Beadle	B30F	1/1948	Ex United Counties O.C. (119). via D.J. Morrison, Tenby, Pembrokeshire (28).	3/1957	11/1964
DBD 940	Bedford OB	73858	Beadle	B30F	3/1948	Ex United Counties O.C. (123). via D.J. Morrison, Tenby, Pembrokeshire (27).	4/1957	4/1963
HCJ 273	Bedford OB	142025	Duple 'Vista'	C29F	8/1950	Ex Baynham. Ross-on-Wye, Herefordshire.	4/1957	8/1964
MUM 790	Bedford OB	120243	Duple 'Vista'	C29F	12/1949	Ex Heaps Tours. Leeds. via D.J. Morrison. Tenby, Pembrokeshire (35).	7/1958	6/1968
HSG 231	Bedford OB	145752	Duple 'Vista'	C29F	10/1950	Ex Halley. Edinburgh. via Pentland. Loanhead, Midlothian.	9/1959	10/1964
SY 9207	Bedford OB	114058	Duple 'Vista'	C29F	9/1949	Ex Allen. Dalkeith, Midlothian. via Russell. Stoneyburn, West Lothian.	by 9/1961 lic.12/1964	7/1967
LUA 541	Bedford OB	68097	Duple 'Vista'	C29F	1/1948	Ex Hudson. Leeds. via D.S. Davies, New Inn, Carmarthenshire.	12/1962	12/1965
ASB 658	Bedford SBG	36564	Duple 'Vega'	C38F	4/1955	Ex Allen. Dalkeith, Midlothian. via Davies. Liverpool.	4/1963	11/1968
JRN 500	Bedford SBG	47098	Plaxton 'Venturer III'	C41F	6/1956	Ex Bon Chaunce, Preston, Lancs via Jones (Reliance Coaches) Llanishen, C'diff.	5/1964	3/1968
JDK 216	Bedford SB	5953	Duple 'Vega'	C33F	3/1952	Ex Boyd. Manchester. via Evans, Senghenydd, and Courtis, Cardiff.	2/1965	9/1968
EUJ 855	Bedford OB	86828	Mulliner	B31F	10/1948	Ex Edwards. Bwlchgwyn, Wrexham. via Roberts. Wellington, Salop.	4/1965	10/1966

Reg	Chassis	Serial	Body	Config	Date	History	In service	Out
BEX 350	Bedford SB3 (SB1 diesel engine)	61721	Duple 'Vega'	C41F	6/1958	Ex Norfolk M.S. Gt Yarmouth (183). via Walker. Hexthorpe, Doncaster.	10/1966	10/1974
HB 7158	Bedford SB (oil)	17299	Burlingham 'Seagull'	C35F	7/1953	Ex Morlais M.S. Merthyr Tydfil (58).	12/1966.	8/1969
HB 7491	Bedford SB (Meadows 4DC engine)	16742	Burlingham 'Seagull'	C35F	5/1953	Ex Morlais M.S. Merthyr Tydfil (57).	1/1967	9/1968
YCV 197	Bedford SBG (SB1 diesel engine)	50894	Duple 'Vega'	C41F	7/1957	Ex Crimson Tours. St Ives, Cornwall. via Rowland. Bilsthorpe, Notts.	7/1967	8/1971
JUO 608	Bedford OB	76097	Duple 'Vista'	C29F	6/1948	Ex Devon General/Grey Cars (TCB608). via Gwyn Williams, Lower Tumble, Llanelli (6).	2/1968	10/1969
YWT 33	Bedford SB1	70489	Plaxton 'Consort IV'	C41F	6/1959	Ex Furness. High Green, Sheffield. via Betts. Wickersley, South Yorkshire.	4/1968	7/1972
125 WRR	Bedford SB13	94952	Duple 'Bella Vega'	C41F	6/1964	Ex Lindrick Coaches. Langold, Notts.	11/1968	6/1975
OKJ 958	Bedford SB	5579	Duple 'Vega'	C33F	10/1951	Ex Ayers. Dover, Kent. via Williams Bros. Upper Tumble. Llanelli.	6/1969	1971
TTH 57	Bedford SB8	70293	Duple Midland	B40F	6/1959	Ex J.A.C. Davies. Felingwm, Carmarthenshire. via Daniel Jones & Sons, Carmarthen (8).	5/1971	7/1976
MUH 140	Leyland 'Tiger Cub' PSUC1/1	565621	Weymann 'Hermes'	B44F	10/1956	Ex Western Welsh O.C. (1140).	5/1971 lic. 6/1971	by 1/1977
6610 PT	Bedford SB1	88002	Yeates 'Pegasus'	DP44F bus seats	10/1961	Ex Bond Bros. Willington, Co Durham. via Edwards. Markham, Gwent.	7/1971	10/1974
STH 800K	Bedford YRQ	2T474749	Duple 'Viceroy Express'	C45F	4/1972	New	lic. 7/1972	6/1987
XTH 700M	Bedford YRQ	DW453847	Duple 'Dominant Exp'	C45F	4/1974	New	4/1974	7/1984
LUN 528F	Bedford SB8	7T457148	Duple 'Bella Vega'	C41F	5/1968	Ex Hanmer. Wrexham, Clwyd.	10/1974	by 11/1983
DRH 122C	Bedford SB5	96651	Plaxton 'Embassy IV'	C41F	4/1965	Ex McMaster. Hull, Yorks. via Cwmbran Motors. Cwmbran, Gwent.	10/1974	3/1982
VCH 165	Leyland 'Tiger Cub' PSUC1/2	606916	Willowbrook	DP41F	4/1961	Ex Trent M.S. (165). via J.H. Davies & Co. (Summerdale Coaches). Letterston, Pembrokeshire.	4/1975	9/1978
HVJ 146N	Bedford YRQ	EW452840	Duple 'Dominant'	B47F	6/1975	New	6/1975	3/1992

Reg	Chassis	Serial	Body	Seating	New	History	In	Out
MBX 381P	Bedford YLQ	FW454214	Duple 'Dominant Express'	C45F	7/1976	New	7/1976	6/1992
NBX 581	Leyland 'Tiger Cub' PSUC1/2T	565253	Willowbrook	DP45F	7/1956	Ex Davies Bros (Pencader) Ltd. (51).	10/1976	9/1978
NFR 837	Bedford SB3 (oil)	58383	Yeates 'Europa'	C41F	2/1958	Ex Blackhurst. Blackpool. via J. Tulk. Brynhyfryd, Swansea. and T.M. Thomas, Capel Dewi, Carmarthen.	by 1/1977	not operated
KHN 730D	Bristol MW6G	233.077	Eastern Coachworks	B45F	8/1966	Ex United Counties Omnibus Co. (U730). via Ribble Motor Services (281).	by 5/1977 lic. 7/1977	8/1979
ATU 56F	Bedford VAL70	7T451225	Plaxton 'Panorama II'	C52F	4/1968	Ex Jackson. Altrincham, Cheshire (56). via Coach Services. Thetford, Norfolk.	10/1977	8/1979
608 CYS	Bedford C5C1	5063	Duple 'Super Vista'	C29F	6/1961	Ex McBrayne. Glasgow (184). via Parish. Morda, Salop.	9/1978	1981
WUX 658K	Bedford YRQ	2T470873	Willowbrook	B49F	12/1971	Ex Brown. Donnington Wood, Salop.	9/1978	11/1983
FFP 200V	Ford R1114	BCRSWC 494180	Duple 'Dominant II'	C53F	8/79	New	8/1979	8/1994
EMB 151K	Ford R226	BCO4LJ 49980	Plaxton 'Panorama Elite II'	C53F	4/1972	Ex Jackson. Altrincham, Cheshire (151). via Elcock & Prince. Ironbridge, Salop.	2/1980 lic. 3/1980	by 9/1982
OBX 125J	Bedford VAS5	OT477536	Willowbrook	B30F	12/1970	Ex Thomas Bros. Llangadog, Carmarthenshire.	1/1981	10/1990
VJU 259X	Ford R1114	BCRSAL 262090	Plaxton 'Supreme VI'	C53F	3/1982	New	3/1982	7/1987
NBX 666R	Bedford YMT	FW453944	Duple 'Dominant'	C53F	9/1976	Ex Richards Bros. Moylegrove, Pembrokeshire.	2/1983	5/1983
VFH 700S	Leyland 'Leopard' PSU3C/4R	7602485	Duple 'Dominant Express'	C53F	9/1977	Ex Pullham. Bourton-on-the-water, Glos.	5/1983	9/1985
LTR 997R	Bedford YMT	FW453685	Plaxton 'Supreme III'	C53F	11/1976	Ex Corinthian. Chandlers Ford, Hants. via Tedd. Thruxton, Hampshire.	8/1983	4/1984
TNP 6V	Volvo B58-56	13834	Caetano 'Alpha'	C53F	1/1980	Ex Halford. Kempsey, Worcs. via Aston. Kempsey, Worcs.	5/1984	1/1987
STT 413R	Bristol LH6L	LH 1370	Eastern Coachworks	B43F	6/1977	Ex Western National O.C. (121). via Devon General (121).	8/1984 lic. 9/1984	6/1996
KUY 442X	Volvo B58-56	15370	Plaxton 'Supreme IV Express'	C53F	3/1982	Ex Halford. Kempsey, Worcs. via Aston. Kempsey, Worcs.	9/1985	6/1996

Above: A superb view of the former Western National, ECW bodied Bristol LH6L, STT 413R, as it left the paintshop of Ffoshelig Garage in August 1984. This vehicle had quite a lengthy stay at Ffoshelig, passing to the new proprietor of Ffoshelig Coaches, Rhodri Evans in June 1996, later passing to Rapson, Brora, Scottish Highlands, for further use, in October 1997. *(Jason Feeley collection).*

Reg	Chassis	Serial	Body	Seating	Date	History	Date in	Date out
D422 JDB	Freight-Rover 350D	267920	Dixon-Lomas 'Made-2-measure'	C16F	8/1986	New	9/1986	8/1990
A233 GNR	Volvo B10M-61	3794	Duple 'Dominant IV'	C57F to C53F 3/87	1/1984	Ex Fowler. Holbeach Drove, Lincs. via Aston. Kempsey, Worcs.	1/1987	6/1996
OJD 54R	Bristol LH6L	LH 1296	Eastern Coachworks	B45F	10/1976	Ex London Transport (BL54). via Sworder. Walkern, Hertfordshire.	3/1987	6/1996
E345 EVH	DAF MB230DKFL615	289138	Duple '340'	C55F	9/1987	New	9/1987	3/1991
E238 MBX	Mercedes-Benz 609D	668063-20-859909	Reeve-Burgess	B20F	2/1988	New	2/1988	6/1996
LBX 861P	Leyland 'Leopard' PSU3C/4R	7503580	Plaxton 'Supreme Express'	C53F	3/1976	Loaned by Davies Bros. Pencader, whilst accident repairs (caused by a Davies Bros bus) were carried out to a Ffoshelig coach.	10/1989	12/1989
UKG 423S	Leyland 'Leopard' PSU3E/2R	7702650	Willowbrook	B51F	4/1978	Ex Rhymney Valley D.C. (23). via Davies Bros (Pencader) Ltd. (220).	7/1990	7/1994
MPG 153P	Leyland 'Leopard' PSU3C/4R	7503462	Duple 'Dominant'	B53F	4/1976	Ex Safeguard. Guildford, Surrey. via Jenkins. Capel Iwan, Carmarthenshire.	7/1991	6/1996
JRT 710N	Bedford YRT	EW457152	Plaxton 'Derwent'	B55F	8/1975	Ex Chambers. Bures, Essex. via Jenkins. Capel Iwan, Carmarthenshire.	7/1991 not lic.	not operated
C826 KBU	Dodge S56	214893	Northern Counties	B18F	7/1986	Ex GM Buses, Greater Manchester (1826).	10/1991	6/1996
XUY 59V	Volvo B58-56	13993	Plaxton 'Supreme IV Express'	C53F	3/1980	Previously registered *MOI 3565*, *HPY 838V*, *6261 TW*. Originally registered *LRH 809V*, with Holt. Newport, East Yorkshire. Acquired via D.R. Morris. Bromyard, Hereford.	3/1992	6/1996
GMS 305S	Leyland 'Leopard' PSU3E/4R	7704788	Alexander 'Y type'	B53F	4/1978	Ex Alexander (Midland) MPE305. via Henley's. Abertillery, Gwent.	10/1994 lic. 12/94	6/1996
M794 MTH	Mercedes-Benz 709D	669003-2N-025150	Mellor	B27F	10/1994	New	10/1994	9/1996

P.R. EVANS (FFOSHELIG COACHES) VEHICLE DETAILS

Reg. No	Chassis make & type	Chassis number	Body make & type	Seating	Date new	Remarks / Additional Information Previous owner	Date acquired	Date withdrawn
YMU 134	Volvo B58-56	15125	Plaxton 'Supreme IV' Fitted with a Plaxton 'Paramount' front end.	C53F	4/1980	Previously reg: *LBU 670V, KIW 3675, LUA 254V*. New to Wallace Arnold, Leeds, as *LUA 254V*. Acquired from J.A. Evans, Tregaron, *before the* Ffoshelig Coaches business was taken over.	9/1995	1/1996
B665 OFP	DAF SB2300DHS585	245131	Plaxton 'Paramount 3200'	C53F	6/1985	Ex Bysiau Cwm Taf, Whitland. Acquired from J.A. Evans, Tregaron, *before the* Ffoshelig Coaches business was taken over.	1/1996	8/1996
XUY 59V	Volvo B58-61	13993	Plaxton 'Supreme IV' Express	C53F	3/1980	Ex D. Jones & Son, Newchurch, Carmarthen, with *part* of the Ffoshelig Coaches business.	6/1996	5/1997
KUY 442X	Volvo B58-56	15370	Plaxton 'Supreme IV' Express	C53F	3/1982	Ex D. Jones & Son, Newchurch, Carmarthen, with *part* of the Ffoshelig Coaches business.	6/1996	4/2001
STT 413R	Bristol LH6L	LH-1370	Eastern Coachworks	B43F	4/1977	Ex D. Jones & Son, Newchurch, Carmarthen, with *part* of the Ffoshelig Coaches business.	6/1996	10/1997
ARR 956Y	Leyland 'Tiger' TRCTL11/3R	8200409	Plaxton 'Supreme V' fitted with 'Paramount' front end.	C50F to C57F 8/97	8/1982	Ex Stott Milnsbridge, West Yorkshire. Previously registered *MSU 433*, originally, *VRA 3Y*.	8/1996	9/1998
NDW 147X	Leyland 'Tiger' TRCTL11/2R	8102831	Plaxton 'Supreme VI' Express	C53F	3/1982	Ex Hills. Tredegar, Gwent, via Smith. Pylle (50). Previously registered *505 AYB*, orig. *NDW 147X*.	8/1996	9/1996
JUH 229W	Leyland 'Leopard' PSU4F/2R	8031228	Duple 'Dominant'	B47F to B53F 8/97 to DP45F 10/98	6/1981	Ex Merthyr Tydfil B.C. (229), via Jones Motors, Login, Carmarthenshire, and J. Williams, Porthcawl Omnibus Co., Porthcawl, Mid-Glam.	11/1996	7/2005
DSU 772 RAZ 9859	Volvo B10M-61	9791	Plaxton 'Paramount 3200' Mk II	C53F to C57F by 10/98	4/1985	Ex Excelsior, Bournemouth, via Lloyd, Bagillt, and Hillman (White Lion Cs) Tredegar, Gwent. Originally registered *B908 SPR*. Re-registered *RAZ 9859*. 4/1998.	5/1997	11/2004
WJB 490 GDE 416W	Leyland 'Leopard' PSU5D/4R	8030768	Plaxton 'Supreme IV'	C57F	11/1980	Ex National Travel (West) 269, via Edwards, Tiers Cross, Pembrokeshire. Previously reg'd: *SVM 475W, WSV 550*, originally, *MRJ 268W*. Re-registered *GDE 416W*. 8/1997.	8/1997	11/1999
JIL 2433	Volvo B10M-61	3778	Plaxton 'Paramount 3500'	C49FT	3/1983	Ex Richmond. Epsom, via Hillman, Tredegar. Previously reg'd: *KXI 366*, originally, *NGT 1Y*.	8/1997	3/2001

Reg	Chassis	Body	Seating	New	History	Acquired	Disposed
E565 UHS **DSU 772** **E857 WEP**	Volvo B10M-61	014950	Plaxton 'Paramount 3500'	C49FT	9/1987	Ex Moffat & Williamson, Gauldry, Fife, Scotland. Previously reg'd: *FSU 375*, originally, *E665 UHS*. Re-registered **DSU 772**, on arrival 4/1998. Re-registered **E857 WEP**, upon sale in 9/1999.	4/1998	9/1999
LIL 9924	Leyland 'Leopard' PSU3G/4R	8230901	Plaxton 'Supreme V' Express	C53F	9/1982	Ex Mayne. Clayton, Greater Manchester (61). Originally registered, *VRC 610Y*.	8/1998	11/2000
JTU 229T	Bedford YLQ	HW457623	Plaxton 'Supreme IV'	C45F	2/1979	Ex J.M. Morgan (Meurig's Coaches) Lampeter.	9/1998	9/1998
ERU 390V	Leyland 'Leopard' PSU3E/4R	7902070	Plaxton 'Supreme IV' Express	C53F	9/1979	Ex Bournemouth B.C. Yellow Buses (90). via Davies Bros (Pencader) Ltd (249).	8/1999	9/1999 not operated
JLJ 109V	Leyland 'Leopard' PSU3E/4R	7930038	Plaxton 'Supreme IV' Express	C53F	5/1980	Ex Bournemouth B.C. (Yellow Buses (109). via Davies Bros (Pencader) Ltd (248).	8/1999	8/1999 not operated
V2 FOS **V35 LDE**	Dennis 'Javelin' 12m	42181	Berkhof 'Axial 50'	C51FT	9/1999	New Re-registered **V35 LDE** upon sale, 1/2001.	9/1999	1/2001
JUI 1720	Leyland 'Tiger' TRCTL11/3R	8103052	Plaxton 'Supreme V'	C57F	5/1982	Ex Safeguard. Guildford. Originally *UPG 349X*. via D.C. Edwards (Bysiau Cwm Taf), Whitland.	11/1999	2/2002
KUI 1372	Volvo B10M-61	13135	Plaxton 'Paramount 3500'	C51F	5/1987	Ex Roberts. Cefn Mawr, Clwyd. via D.C. Edwards (Bysiau Cwm-Taf), Whitland. Previously: *D185 KDE, 526 NDE, D327 UTU, VLT 191, VLT 290*, originally: *D290 UDM*.	5/2000	9/2002
A10 SBK **TIL 4527**	Leyland 'Tiger' TRCL10/3ARZM	TR00295	Plaxton 'Paramount 3500'	C49FT	6/1988	Ex Isaac & Morgan (G&M Coaches) Lampeter. Previously registered: *E882 HFW, PS 2743*, originally registered, *E510 RFU*. Re-registered **TIL 4527**, 3/2002.	1/2001	8/2005
JLJ 109V	Leyland 'Leopard' PSU3E/4R	7930038	Plaxton 'Supreme IV' Express.	C53F	5/1980	Ex Davies Coaches, Llanelli.	3/2001	1/2002
M326 KRY **DSU 772**	Volvo B10M-62	42416	Jonckheere 'Deauville 45'	C53F	4/1995	Ex Clarkes. Lower Sydenham, London. Re-registered **DSU 772**, on arrival. 3/2001. Re-registered **M326 KRY**, upon sale. 9/2010.	3/2001	9/2010
KXI 318	Volvo B10M-61	3784	Plaxton 'Supreme V'	C57F	6/1982	Ex Hillman (White Lion Coaches), Tredegar. Previously reg'd: *YHR 702*, originally: *TND 431X*.	2/2002	8/2004
HIL 2329	Volvo B10M-61	3788	Plaxton 'Supreme V'	C53F	7/1982	Ex Hillman (White Lion Coaches), Tredegar. Previously *BUA 161X, 9778 WA, VMX 363X*.	4/2002	4/2004
IIL 8521	Toyota 'Coaster' HDB30R	0001455	Caetano 'Optimo II'	C21F	11/1991	Ex Williams Coaches. Brecon, Powys. Previously registered, *J234 HVK*.	7/2002	5/2004

Reg	Chassis	Chassis no.	Body	Seating	New	History	Acquired	Disposal
D345 KVE **MUI 7389**	Volvo B10M-61	13870	Van-Hool 'Alizee T8'	C53F	4/1987	Ex Kime. Folkingham, Lincolnshire. Re-registered *MUI 7389*, 1/2003.	11/2002	7/2005
R91 GWO	Mercedes-Benz 'Vario' 0814D	6703742N-064734	Autobus 'Nouvelle 2'	C29F	1/1998	Ex Bebb. Llantwit Fardre, Pontypridd. via Miles, Stratton-St Margaret, Wiltshire.	8/2004	8/2005
CV02 LTA	Volkswagen Transporter	WV1ZZZ70Z2H062648	Cymric Conversions	-?-	7/2002	Ex Private owner @ Newport. Gwent,	9/2004 Non PSV	8/2006
T255 GON **YSU 366**	Kassbohrer-Setra S315GT-HD	32600001-015023	Kassbohrer-Setra	C48FT	7/1999	Ex Parry. Cheslyn Hay, Staffs. via Silver Star. Caernarfon, Gwynedd. Re-registered *YSU 366*, on arrival. 9/2004.	9/2004	12/2009
A475 TBX	Volvo B10M-61	06957	Plaxton 'Paramount 3200'	C57F	3/1984	Ex Jones Motors. Login, Carmarthenshire. Previously reg'd, *YDE 679*, originally, *A475 TBX*.	8/2005	7/2015
R6 HLC	Scania L94IB4	YS4L4X20001831563	Irizar 'Intercentury'	C57F	4/1998	Ex Lucketts. Fareham, Hants. via Roadliner. Poole, Dorset. Previously reg'd, *R555 ELF*, originally *R6 HLC*.	8/2005	10/2006
L975 VDE	DAF 400	CN 942534	Autobus Classique	16 to -7-	3/1994	Ex Jones Motors. Login, Carmarthenshire. via Davies Coaches. Llanelli, Carmarthenshire.	8/2005 Non PSV	8/2006
FF05 BUS **CV55 MVM**	Mercedes-Benz 'Vario' 0814D	WDB6703742N118332	Plaxton 'Cheetah'	C33F	9/2005	New Re-registered *CV55 MVM* upon sale, 7/2011.	9/2005	7/2011
SCD 693X	Leyland 'Leopard' PSU3F/5R	8030394	Plaxton 'Supreme V'	C53F	10/1981	Ex Alpha Coaches. Brighton. via F.E. Lewis. Whitland, Carmarthenshire.	6/2006	8/2011
MX53 ZWD	Mercedes-Benz 'Vario' 0814D	WDB6703732N111952	Onyx	C24F	12/2003	Ex Hutchinson. Easingwold, N. Yorkshire. via F.E. Lewis. Whitland, Carmarthenshire.	6/2006	10/2008
YN53 VBO	Mercedes-Benz 'Vario' 0814D	WDB6703742N111612	Plaxton 'Beaver 2'	B33F	1/2004	Ex Cresswell. Evesham, Worcestershire. via: F.E. Lewis. Whitland, Carmarthenshire.	6/2006	8/2006
JUI 5931	Volvo B10M-60	031242	Van-Hool 'Alizee T8'	C49FT	3/1993	Ex Wallace Arnold. Leeds. via Isaac & Morgan (G&M Coaches) Lampeter. Originally registered, *K818 HUM*.	8/2006	7/2007
N50 PDE **VIL 9911**	Volvo B10M-62	YV31M2F10TA045167	Van-Hool 'Alizee T8'	C53F	5/1996	Ex New Bharat. Southall, London. via Edwards. Tiers Cross, Pembrokeshire. Originally registered, *N21 EYB*. Re-registered *VIL 9911*, 4/2007.	11/2006	10/2008
BU56 OOD	Optare 'Solo' M990	SABGWFAE06L192546	Optare	B37F	11/2006	New	11/2006	4/2011
MX04 VLT	Optare 'Solo' M850	1900000-0001310	Optare	B29F	4/2004	Demonstrator, operated on loan from Optare, (dealer), Crossgates, Leeds.	11/2006	11/2006

Reg	Chassis	Serial	Body	Seating	Date	Notes	Acquired	Disposed
G828 XWS *YIL 8181*	Leyland 'Tiger' TRCTL11/3LZM	TR00784	Plaxton 'Derwent II'	DP68F 3+2 seating	11/1989	Ex Ministry of Defence, *03 KJ 30*. via Eurotaxis, Siston Common, Bristol. Re-registered *YIL 8181*, 4/2007.	2/2007	7/2009
YJ07 EGD	Optare 'Tempo' X1260	6L280038	Optare		B46F	3/2007	Demonstrator, operated on hire from dealer, Optare, Crossgates, Leeds.	7/2007	7/2007
RE57 FOS	Alexander-Dennis 'Javelin' 12 metre	SFD745BR 55GJ22600	Plaxton 'Profile'	C57F	9/2007	New	9/2007	Current
YJ57 BTZ	VDL SB4000 12 metre	XMGDE40X S0H014617	Van-Hool 'Alizee T9'	C51FT	9/2007	Hired from Arriva Bus & Coach, Cleckheaton. See note on page 167.	7/2008	10/2008
G829 XWS	Leyland 'Tiger' TRCTL11/3LZM	TR00780	Plaxton 'Derwent II'	B70F	11/1989	Ex Ministry of Defence, *03 KJ 23*. via Eurotaxis, *G829 XWS*, *818 CHW*, *G829 XWS*, and Davies Coaches, Llanelli (not operated).	9/2007	7/2009
Y586 TOV *V2 FOS* *Y586 TOV*	Kassbohrer-Setra S315GT-HD	WKK32600- 001015108	Kassbohrer-Setra	C53F	4/2001	Ex Clarkes, Lower Sydenham, London. Re-registered *V2 FOS*, 11/2008. Re-registered *Y586 TOV* upon sale, 10/2013.	10/2008	10/2013
PUI 3785	Volvo B10M-60	YV31MGD1 8KA020370	Van-Hool 'Alizee T8'	C53F	3/1989	Ex Dawlish Coaches, Dawlish, Devon. Previously registered *F512 LTT*.	10/2008	7/2010
M734 BSJ	Volvo B6-50	YV3R36E18 RC005642	Alexander 'Dash'	DP40F	10/1994	Ex Western Scottish (V334). via Ridgeway, Port Talbot, West Glam.	11/2008	9/2009
BX56 XAL *DS56 FOS* *BX56 XAL*	Autosan 'Eagle' A1012T	SUAEDCPP 55620186	Autosan	C67F	9/2006	Ex Goulden, Welwyn Garden City (72). Re-registered *DS56 FOS*, 4/2009. Re-registered *BX56 XAL* upon sale, 8/2015.	2/2009 lic. 4/2009	8/2015
R705 MNU	Volvo B10M-62	YV31MA611 VA046762	Plaxton 'Premiere 320'	C57F	10/1997	Ex Ken Hopkins, Tonna, West Glam (191). Previously reg'd. *WYM 675*, originally *R705 MNU*.	7/2009	8/2009
WD03 WWW *B6 PRE* *WD03 WWW*	Volvo B7R	YV3R6G711 3A005494	Jonckheere 'Modulo'	C55F	5/2003	Ex O'Shea, Ballyheigue, Co Kerry as 03-KY-2698 (Dealer re-registered to WD03 WWW by 6/2007) via Hilton, Newton-le-Willows, Merseyside. Re-registered *B6 PRE*, 9/2010. Re-registered *WD03 WWW* upon sale, 8/2017.	8/2009	8/2017
YJ59 NMZ	Optare 'Versa' V1100	-L320245	Optare	B38F	11/2009	New	11/2009	7/2013
VU03 ZPS	Mercedes-Benz 'Vario' 0814D	WDB670374 2N109208	Plaxton 'Beaver 2'	DP33F	4/2003	Hired from 'Next Bus', Chippenham, Wilts.	11/2009	3/2010
YJ59 NNY	Optare 'Solo' M710SE	SABCN2AB 09L193556	Optare	B21F	1/2010	New	1/2010	1/2019

P501 RYM	Dennis 'Dart' SLF	SFD112BRI TGW10420	Plaxton 'Pointer 2'	B32F	11/1996	Ex London General (LDP1).	3/2010	2/2011
EJ52 UYS DSU 772 EJ52 UYS	Volvo B10M-62	YV31MA612 1A052693	Van-Hool 'Alizee T9'	C49FT	10/2002	New to Richmond. Barley, Herts, as 649 ETF. (Re-registered EJ52 UYS by Richmond, in 2010). Acquired from Richmond, 8/2010. re-registered DSU 772 when licenced in 9/2010, returning to EJ52 UYS, 12/2017, pending sale.	8/2010	3/2018
N711 AHP	Volvo B10M-62	YV31M2B15 SA043080	Plaxton 'Premiere 350'	C70F	12/1995	Ex Bus Eireann, Irish Republic (VP9) 95-D-41599 (Dealer re-registered to N711 AHP, in 12/1999). via Llynfi Coaches. Maesteg, Mid-Glam.	9/2010	10/2014
DS11 FOS	Mercedes-Benz 'Vario' 0816D	WDB670374 2N141419	Plaxton 'Cheetah'	C33F	4/2011	New	4/2011	Current
X847 XDE	Dennis 'Javelin'	SFD725BR4 YGJ22331	Plaxton 'Premiere 320'	C70F	2/2001	Ex Jones Motors. Login, Carmarthenshire.	8/2011	8/2016
X848 XDE	Dennis 'Javelin'	SFD725BR4 YGJ22332	Plaxton 'Premiere 320'	C70F	2/2001	Ex Jones Motors. Login, Carmarthenshire.	8/2011	8/2016
YJ06 YSG	Optare 'Solo' M950	SAB190000 00002270	Optare	B33F	5/2006	Dealer loan from Optare, Sherburn-in-Elmet.	11/2011	11/2011
P564 PNE	Mercedes-Benz 'Vario' 0814D	WDB670374 2N064195	Plaxton 'Beaver 2'	B27F	7/1997	Ex John Morrow. Glasgow.	4/2012	10/2012
MP51 BUZ	Optare 'Solo' M850	SAB190000 00000660	Optare	B27F	10/2001	Ex John Morrow. Glasgow. Previously reg'd B15 EDC, originally, MP51 BUZ.	4/2012	10/2013
SF55 PSY	Mercedes-Benz 'Vario' 0814D	WDB670374 2N117496	Plaxton 'Beaver 2'	DP29FL	10/2005	Ex Chapman. New Stevenston, Lanarkshire.	8/2013	8/2019
YJ08 ECX FF05 BUS YJ08 ECX	VDL SB4000	XMGDE40P SOH014783	Berkhof 'Axial 50'	C53F	6/2008	Ex BM Coaches. Hayes, London. via Golden Tours. Victoria, London. Re-registered FF05 BUS, 10/2013. Returned to YJ08 ECX, 1/2016, pending sale.	10/2013	2/2016
FN09 AOA V2 FOS	Volvo B7R (10metre)	YV3R6K625 9A130424	Sunsundegui 'Sideral'	C44F	5/2009	Ex Priory City of Lincoln Acadamy. Re-registered V2 FOS, 7/2014.	7/2014	Current
YJ55 YGX	Optare 'Solo' M850SL	SAB190000 00002133	Optare	B23F	11/2005	Ex Compass. Worthing, West Sussex.	9/2014	12/2018
M326 KRY XUD 367	Volvo B10M-62	42416	Jonckheere 'Deauville 45'	C53F	4/1995	Re-acquired ex Davies Coaches. Llanelli, Previously reg'd JIL 7567, originally M326 KRY. Re-registered XUD 367, 8/2016.	2/2015	4/2018

Reg	Model	Chassis	Body	Seats	New	Notes	Acquired	Disposed
YV07 PVJ DS56 FOS YV07 PVJ	Volvo B7R	YV3R6K6247A121078	Plaxton 'Profile'	C57F to C70F	12/2007	Ex Ministry of Defence, NU07 YGH, via Snaith, Otterburn, Northumberland. Re-registered DS56 FOS, 9/2015. Re-registered YV07 PVJ, 3/2020.	8/2015	3/2020
RE65 FOS	Mercedes-Benz 'Tourismo M'	WEB63241523000570	Mercedes-Benz	C55F	1/2016	New	1/2016	Current
BL16 FYV	Mercedes-Benz 'Tourismo M'	WEB63247523000750	Mercedes-Benz	C57FT	5/2016	Demonstrator on loan from Evobus (dealer), Coventry.	8/2016	8/2016
OU16 EWW	Auwarter-Neoplan 'N2216/35HDC'	WAGP20ZZ3GT022948	Neoplan 'Tourliner P20'	C55FT	5/2016	Demonstrator on loan from MAN, Trafford Park.	9/2016	9/2016
BV55 FPN FF05 BUS	Kassbohrer-Setra S416GT-HD	WKK63213423100966	Kassbohrer (Integral)	C53FT	2/2006	Ex Kings Ferry Coaches. Gillingham, Kent. via Lodge, High Easter, Essex. Previously reg'd 46 AEW, originally BV55 FPN. Re-registered FF05 BUS, 9/2016.	8/2016	Current
YN54 DDV	Mercedes-Benz 'Vario' 0814D	WDB6703742N113630	Plaxton 'Cheetah'	C33F	9/2004	Ex Apple Travel. Slough. Bucks. Previously reg'd T33 APL, originally YN54 DDV.	9/2017	8/2018
WA11 HXL B6 PRE	VDL (Bova) 'Futura' FHD127.365	XL9AA38RB34003974	VDL 'Futura' (Integral)	C54FT	6/2011	Ex Hillier (Hatts Coaches), Foxham, Wilts. via Williams Coaches. Brecon, Powys. Re-registered B6 PRE, 12/2017.	12/2017	Current
YN58 CFX B10 PRE	Dennis 'Javelin'	SFD755BR68GJ22608	Plaxton 'Profile'	C70F	10/2008	Ex Swans Travel. Chadderton, Oldham. Re-registered B10 PRE, 9/2018.	9/2018	Current
YN60 FMG DSU 772	Dennis 'Javelin'	SFD765BR7AGJ22666	Plaxton 'Profile'	C70F	11/2010	Ex Roy McCarthy Coaches. Macclesfield. Re-registered DSU 772, 11/2018.	10/2018	Current
BF67 WLK	Mercedes-Benz 'Tourismo M/3'	WEB41056523001140	Mercedes-Benz	C57FT	2/2018	Demonstrator on loan from Evobus (dealer), Coventry.	12/2018	1/2020
YN59 BMO	ADL "Javelin'	SFD755BR69GJ22637	Plaxton 'Profile'	C57F	12/2009	Ex Roy McCarthy Coaches. Macclesfield.	5/2019	Current
K51 TER	Volvo B10M-60	YV31M2B12PA031038	Van-Hool 'Alizee T8'	C50FT	3/1993	Ex Kenzies Coaches. Shepreth, Cambridge.	9/2019	Current
MIG 1727	Dennis 'Javelin'	SFD721BR41GJ22345	Plaxton 'Prima'	C55F	2002	Ex Ministry of Defence, MU51 FDJ. via Swansea Bus & Coach Co, & re-registered CP51 ZBE, & MIG 1727, and via M. Hayward, dealer/operator, Carmarthen.	11/2019	10/2020
SN53 ETR	Transbus 'Dart' SLF	SFD6BACR33GW87401	Transbus 'Pointer'	B29F	11/2003	Operated on loan from Morris Travel, Carmarthen.	10/2019	10/2019

KP51 SXV	Dennis 'Dart' SLF	SFD6B2CR 31GW15992	Alexander 'ALX200'	B29F	12/2001	Operated on loan from Morris Travel, Carmarthen.	10/2019	10/2019
BU51 FXF XUD 367	Kassbohrer-Setra S315GT-HD	WKK627252 13000133	Kassbohrer-Setra	C49FT	1/2002	New to Welsh's Coaches. Upton, W. Yorkshire. Ex Jones International, Llandeilo, Carms. via Hayward. Carmarthen. Re-registered XUD 367, 11/2020.	10/2020	Current
NDE 916R	Bristol LH6L	LH1309	Eastern Coachworks	B45F	2/1977	Acquired for continued preservation from D. Wita, (Preservationist). Ammanford. This vehicle was new to Daniel Jones & Sons Ltd, Carmarthen, passing to Davies Bros., in April 1978, with the Daniel Jones' business.	22/4/2021 not licenced	Current

ADDITIONAL INFORMATION

The VDL SB4000, registered YJ57 BTZ, was hired from Arriva Bus & Coach, Cleckheaton, from July - October 2008, to cover a vehicle shortage, after the Kassbohrer-Setra, YSU 366, sustained extensive rear-end damage in a collision with a First Group 'Rail Air' Irizar bodied coach, on the M4 Motorway near London, 6th June, 2008. No passengers were injured in the accident, but the damage sustained to YSU 366, included all of the rear end 'integral' framework, fan, compressor and body panelling. The repairs, which took four months, were carried out by Full Circle Enterprises Ltd, and all paid for by 'First Group', including the hire of a replacement coach, YJ57 BTZ.

The cherished registration mark, DS56 FOS, is currently still owned by Ffoshelig Coaches, on retention.

PLEASE NOTE

All known vehicle details, are correct to September 2021.

D. JONES (FFOSHELIG COACHES) VEHICLE DISPOSALS

BX 1277	Unknown
Daimler	Unknown
BX 7410	Sold to G. Gimblett (Gimblett Motor Services), Llanelly, date unknown.
TX 8120	Sold to H.E. Clarke. Capel Evan, Newcastle Emlyn, 5/1941, last licensed 1943.
TH 1209	No further trace.
TH 2510	Sold to Evans & Walters, Kilgetty, Pembs. 5/1941. To Richards Bros. Moylegrove, Pembs, 7/1941.
TH 9099	Sold to D.T. Jones, (Marion Jane Jones), Llain, Penybont, Carms, 11/1952. Originally Jones, Trelech, returning to Trelech by 2/1953. Withdrawn 8/1954. To John Evans & Sons. Bancffosfelyn, Pontyberem.
BTH 777	No further trace.
CBX 160	No further trace.
CTH 555	No further trace.
TH 4455	No further trace.
SX 5144	No further trace.
ACJ 968	Sold to Thomas Bros. Llangadock (Llangadog) Carms. -/1950. To George Wm. West. Burry Port, Carms. 9/1951, & sold by 1955. Noted in use as a mobile caravan by 1958.
DTH 999	Scrapped at garage by 9/1961.
EBX 666	No further trace.
DWN 256	No further trace.
ETH 888	No further trace.
FDE 623	No further trace.
LPU 620	Out of use at depot 11/1965.
DBD 936	Out of use at depot 3/1965. Broken up by 8/1965.
DBD 940	Being used for spares 5/1963, derelict remains still at depot 3/1965.
HCJ 273	Out of use at depot 8/1965. Being used for spares by 1/1968.
MUM 790	No further trace.
HSG 231	No further trace.
SY 9207	Sold to Perrett. Shipton Oliffe, Gloucestershire, 8/1967.
LUA 541	Used for spares, derelict remains were still at the depot 1/1968.
ASB 658	Sold to Jefferies. Chagford, Devon, 1/1969.
JRN 500	Sold to Kirkby (dealer) South Anston, 4/1968. To Gladwin. Middlesbrough, North Yorkshire, 7/1968.
JDK 216	No further trace.
EUJ 855	Used for spares. Remains were still at the depot 1/1968.
BEX 350	Derelict at depot 6/1976.
HB 7518	No further trace.
HB 7491	In use as a seat store by 4/1972. Scrapped at depot 8/1974.
YCV 197	Derelict at garage 4/72 & 6/76. Scrapped by 10/1976.
JUO 608	Sold to The West of England Transport Collection, Winkleigh, Devon, 5/1971. Still recorded at DVLA.
YWT 33	Derelict at depot by 8/1974.
125 WRR	Sold to Owen. Knighton, Powys, 8/1975.
OKJ 958	In use as office at the garage by 8/1972, still there 2/1980. Gone for scrap by 8/1981.
TTH 57	Sold to Greenhous (dealer) Hereford, 7/1976. To Middleton Metals (scrap dealer) Ludlow, 8/1976.
MUH 140	Used for spares by 1/1977, and used as a store shed by 2/1980. Sold for scrap 11/1980.
6610 PT	Sold to Greenhous (dealer) Hereford, 10/1974. To Mid-Wales Motors, Newtown, for spares by 6/1975.
STH 800K	Sold to Morrison. Crynant, West Glamorgan, 6/1987.
XTH 700M	Sold to dealer for export to Malta, 7/1984. To E. Galea, Gzira, Malta, entered service as Y-1112, 11/1984, re-reg. Y- 0411, later **DBY 411**. Withdrawn 7/2011. To Tar-Robba for scrap, and scrapped by 10/2011.
LUN 528F	Out of use at depot 11/1984, still there 1/1990. Scrapped by 12/1992.
DRH 122C	Scrapped by 7/1984.
VCH 165	Sold to Greenhous (dealer) Hereford, 9/1978. To Evans. Shifnal, Salop. 10/1978.
HVJ 146N	Sold to J.A. Evans. Tregaron. 3/1992. To D.C. Edwards. (Bysiau Cwm-Taf), Whitland, 3/1992.
MBX 381P	Sold to J.M. Morgan, Lampeter, Ceredigion, 6/1992. To J.A. Evans. Tregaron, Ceredigion, 4/1998.

Above: The disposal for Jones, Ffoshelig's Duple 'Dominant I' bodied Bedford YRQ, **XTH 700M**, is confirmed by this view of it taken in Malta, where it was firstly registered Y-1112, then Y-0411 and finally DBY 411 as shown.

Above: When Des Jones, Ffoshelig, sold this Bedford YLQ, **MBX 381P**, to Meurig Morgan, Lampeter, in June 1992, Meurig retained the Ffoshelig Coaches' livery of mid-cream and brown, as shown. *(V. Morgan).*

NBX 581	Sold to Greenhous (dealer) Hereford, 9/1978. To Dilevent. Bromyard, Hereford 10/1978.
NFR 837	Not operated. Acquired for spares only, and subsequently scrapped.
KHN 730D	Sold to E. Beckett (scrap dealer) Dunscroft, Doncaster, S. Yorkshire, 8/1979.
ATU 56F	Sold to J.G. Simmons. Maesteg, Mid-Glamorgan, 8/1979. Later G. Rees & J.G. Simmons.
608 CYS	For sale 6/1981, still owned 8/1981, sold by 4/1982. No further trace.
WUX 658K	Sold to Richards Bros. Moylegrove, Dyfed (Pembs), 11/1983. (Richards Bros. Cardigan, from 3/1985).
FFP 200V	Sold to Rees (Midway Motors) Crymych, Dyfed (Pembs) 8/1994. Sold for caravan conversion 7/2005.
EMB 151K	Sold to J.A. Evans. Tregaron, Dyfed, by 9/1982. To D.W. & W.S. Rees (Mid-Way Motors), Crymych, with accident damage for spares, by 7/1984.
OBX 125J	Sold to J.M. Morgan (Meurigs Coaches) Lampeter, Dyfed, 10/1990. To J.A. Evans, Tregaron, 3/1991, not operated, sold for mobile caravan conversion to unknown owner at Lampeter, and noted for sale in 2010.
VJU 259X	Sold to Davies & Jones (Summerdale Coaches), Letterston, Dyfed, 7/1987. Withdrawn 7/2000, and scrapped on site by 8/2003.
NBX 666R	Sold to Richards Bros. Moylegrove, Dyfed (Pembs), the original owners, in 5/1983. Note, this vehicle had retained its Richards Bros. livery throughout its 3 month stay at Ffoshelig.
VFH 700S	Sold to Rees & Williams. Tycroes, Dyfed (Carms), 9/1985. Passing to D Coaches, Morriston, Swansea, with the R&W business 8/1987. To T. Wigley, Carlton dealer, for scrap, 8/1996.
LTR 997R	Sold to James Bros. Llangeithio, Dyfed (Ceredigion), 4/1984. Withdrawn by 3/2000, with no further trace.
TNP 6V	Sold to Telford. Highworth, Wilts, 1/1987. To O'sullivan. Huyton, Merseyside, 4/1990, as **IIW 4582**.
STT 413R	Sold to Rhodri Evans, Carmarthen, 6/1996, with the main portion of the Ffoshelig business. To Rapson. Brora, Scottish Highlands, 10/1997.
KUY 442X	Sold to Rhodri Evans, Carmarthen, 6/1996, with the main portion of the Ffoshelig business. To J.A. Evans, Tregaron, Ceredigion, 4/2001. To Keith Jones. Blaengarw, Mid-Glam, 4/2001.
D422 JDB	Sold to J.M. Morgan (Meurigs Coaches), Lampeter, Dyfed, 8/1990. To E.J. James. Burry Port, Carms, 7/1993. To Gorslas Mini-bus Hire, Gorslas, Carmarthenshire, 3/1997.
A233 GNR	Sold to F.E. Lewis, Whitland, Carmarthenshire, 6/1996, with part of the Ffoshelig business. To Edwards, (Bysiau Cwm-Taf) Whitland, 1/1999. To J.A. Evans. Tregaron 1/2002. To Price. Newcastle, Salop, 3/2002.
OJD 54R	Sold to Edwards. Tiers Cross, Pembrokeshire, 6/1996. Withdrawn 8/1997, to Carter. Ipswich, 1/1998.
E345 EVH	Sold to Messenger. Aspatria, Cumbria, 3/1991.
E238 MBX	Sold to Richards Bros. Cardigan, 6/1996. Scrapped 10/2008.
LBX 861P	Returned to Davies Bros (Pencader) Ltd, 'off loan' 12/1989.
UKG 423S	Sold to Davies Bros (Pencader) Ltd, 7/1994, (re-united with its previous owner, using the same f/n: 220).
MPG 153P	Sold to F.E. Lewis, Whitland, Carmarthenshire, 6/1996, with part of the Ffoshelig business. To Gwyn Williams & Sons, Lower. Tumble, Carms, (159), 12/1999. Re-registered **GIW 2269** – 3/2000.
JRT 710N	Not operated. Sold to J.A. Evans, Tregaron, Ceredigion, 7/1991. To Owen. Nefyn, Gwynedd, 8/1991.
C826 KBU	Sold to M. Meyers. Llanpumpsaint, Carmarthenshire, 6/1996. Withdrawn by 12/1998, with no further trace.
XUY 59V	Sold to Rhodri Evans, Carmarthen, 6/1996, with the main portion of the Ffoshelig business.
GMS 305S	Sold to F.E. Lewis, Whitland, Carmarthenshire, 6/1996, with part of the Ffoshelig business. To Martin Perry, Bromyard, Hereford, 9/1998.
M794 MTH	Sold to Castle Garages, Llandovery, Carmarthenshire, 6/1996, with part of the Ffoshelig business. To Cross Gates Coaches. Cross Gates, Powys, 9/1998. Withdrawn 7/2007, with no further trace.

Note: It's believed that most of the company's withdrawn Bedford OWB/OB/SBs which are listed as disposed of with 'no further trace' were dismantled for useful spares, and their chassis' were sold locally, for conversion into farm trailers.

One local person, who manufactured these farm trailers from old commercial vehicle chassis, was also a local public service vehicle operator, David Thomas Jones, of Sunnybridge Garage, Abercych, and formerly of Trelech. D.T. Jones was the operator mentioned on page 32, who acquired David Jones' Wednesday only Post Gwyn to Carmarthen service, in October 1963.

P.R. EVANS (FFOSHELIG COACHES) VEHICLE DISPOSALS

YMU 134	Sold To J.A. Evans. Tregaron, Ceredigion. 1/1996. To Wilson. Ratby, Leics. 3/1996.
B665 OFP	Sold to Mid-West Coach Sales (dealer), Cheltenham, 8/1996. To Rich. Croydon, Surrey, 9/1996.
XUY 59V	Sold to J.A. Evans. Tregaron, 5/1997. To Clive Edwards (Bysiau Cwm-Taf) Whitland, 5/1997.
KUY 442X	Sold to J.A. Evans. Tregaron, 4/2001. To Keith Jones (Travel Final), Blaengarw, Mid-Glam, 4/2001.
STT 413R	Sold to Rapson. Brora, Scottish Highlands, 10/1997. To T. Partridge. Saltash, Cornwall for preservation, 6/2005, believed scrapped 2007.
ARR 956Y	Sold to Tonna Luxury Coaches. Tonna, West Glam. (163), 9/1998. Re-registered **XJI 4840**, 12/1998.
NDW 147X	Sold to Thomas & Pugh (t/a Williams Bros), Upper Tumble, Carmarthenshire, (30), 9/1996.
JUH 229W	Sold to Silver Star. Caernarfon, Gwynedd, 7/2005. To T. Wigley (dealer), Carlton, for scrap 4/2007.
DSU 772 **RAZ 9859**	Re-registered **RAZ 9859** - 4/1998. Sold to Edwards Bros. Tiers Cross, Pembrokeshire 11/2004, with the cherished registration, but re-registered **526 NDE** in 8/2006.
WJB 490 **GDE 416W**	Re-registered **GDE 416W** - 8/1997 and the registration **WJB 490**, returned to its previous owner. Sold to Tonna Luxury Coaches, Tonna, West Glam. (168), 11/1999. Re-registered **SIL 4275**, 1/2000
JIL 2433	Sold to Davies Coaches. Llanelli, 3/2001. To Tanners Coaches, Newport, Gwent, 3/2007, without the cherished registration.
E565 UHS **DSU772** **E857 WEP**	Re-registered **DSU 772** before entering service in 4/1998. Re-registered **E857 WEP** upon sale, 9/1999. Sold to Berkhof UK (dealer) Basingstoke, Hants, 9/1999. To Hookways. Meeth, Devon, 11/1999.
LIL 9924	Sold to Morris Travel. Carmarthen, 11/2000, with the cherished registration. Withdrawn by Morris Travel 12/2002, and re-registered to its original registration, **VRC 610Y** - 5/2003.
JTU 229T	Stripped of useful spares & seats, remains to Hayward, Carmarthen, for scrap - 10/1998.
ERU 390V	**Not operated.** Sold to Jones International, Llandeilo, Carms, 9/1999. To A.A. Thomas. Gorseinon, Swansea, 11/1999. Returning to Jones International, Llandeilo for spares by 4/2001.
JLJ 109V	**Not operated.** Sold to K.A. Davies (Davies Coaches), Llanelli, 8/1999, but re-acquired by Rhodri Evans, (Ffoshelig Cs), in 3/2001, returning again to Davies Coaches, Llanelli, 1/2002. Burned out 3/2004.
V2 FOS **V35 LDE**	Re-registered **V35 LDE** - 1/2001, upon sale to Isaac & Morgan (G & M Coaches), Lampeter, Ceredigion, 1/2001.
JUI 1720	Sold to Morris Travel, Carmarthen, 2/2002, re-registered **UPG 349X** - 11/2007. To Hayward for scrap 11/09.
KUI 1372	Sold to Matthews. New Inn, Pontypool, Gwent, 9/2002. To A2Z. Walsall, West Midlands 6/2007.
A10 SBK **TIL 4527**	Re-registered **TIL 4527** - 3/2002. Sold to M. Hayward. Carmarthen, with the cherished registration, 7/2005.
JLJ 109V	Sold to Davies Coaches. Llanelli, for the second time in 1/2002, where it burned out in a mysterious fire at the new depot in Cwmgwili, Llanelli, 3/2004.
M326 KRY **DSU 772** **M326 KRY**	Re-registered **DSU 772** before entering service in 3/2001. Re-registered **M326 KRY** - 8/2010, pending its sale. To Davies Coaches. Llanelli, in 9/2010. Note: this vehicle returned to Ffoshelig Coaches in 2/2015.
KXI 318	Sold to Davies Coaches. Llanelli, with the cherished registration, in 8/2004. Re-registered to its original registration mark, **TND 431X**, by Davies Coaches in 1/2008.
HIL 2329	Sold to its previous owner, Hillman (White Lion Coaches), Tredegar, Gwent, in 4/2004.
IIL 8521	Sold to McKnight (Brook Cars), Laugharne, 4/2004.
D345 KVE **MUI 7389**	Re-registered **MUI 7389** - 1/2003. Sold to Silver Star. Caernarfon, Gwynedd, 7/2005, with the cherished registration.
R91 GWO	Sold to Davies Coaches. Cwmgwili, Llanelli, 8/2005.
CV02 LTA	Sold to unknown private owner, 8/2006.
T255 GON **YSU 366**	Re-registered **YSU 366** - 11/2004. Sold to Eckford's Travel. Hawkinge, Kent, 12/2009, with the cherished registration.
A475 TBX	Sold to Fowler. Holbeach Grove, Lincs, 7/2015.
R6 HLC	Sold to Isaac & Morgan (G & M Coaches), Lampeter, Ceredigion, 10/2006.
L975 VDE	Sold to a private owner at Llanelli, 8/2006, and converted into a 'Mobile Snack Bar' by 5/2007.
FF05 BUS **CV55 MVM**	Re-registered **CV55 MVM**, upon sale, 7/2011. Sold to J.A.G. Hicks (Glyn's Coaches), Mynydd-Cerrig, Carmarthenshire, 7/2011.

SCD 693X	Withdrawn 8/2011. Sold to Alan Dixon. Annfield Plain, Co Durham, 2/2012, for preservation.
MX53 ZWD	Sold to G & M Coaches, Lampeter, Ceredigion, 10/2008. To F.E. Lewis, Whitland, 11/2009. To J.A.G. Hicks (Glyn's), Mynydd-Cerrig, Carmarthenshire, 10/2011.
YN53 VBO	Sold to Davies (Graham's), Tredegar, Gwent, 8/2006.
JUI 5931	Sold to Davies Coaches. Llanelli, 7/2007, with cherished registration.
N50 PDE	Re-registered VIL 9911 - 4/2007.
VIL 9911	Sold to Gwyn Williams Coaches (182), Lr Tumble, Carmarthenshire, 10/2008, with cherished registration.
BU56 OOD	Sold to Plaxton Coach Sales (dealer) 4/2011. To APL Travel. Crudwell, Malmesbury, Wilts. 6/2011.
MX04 VLT	Returned to Optare (dealer), Crossgates, Leeds, ex loan, 11/2006. Sold to Silcox. Pembroke Dock, 6/2007.
G828 XWS	Re-registered YIL 8181 - 4/2007.
YIL 8181	Sold to Gwyn Williams Coaches (184), Lr Tumble, Carmarthenshire, 7/2009, with cherished registration.
YJ07 EGD	Returned to Optare (dealer), Crossgates, Leeds, ex demonstration loan, 7/2007.
RE57 FOS	Current
YJ57 BTZ	Returned to Arriva Bus & Coach (dealer), Cleckheaton, ex loan, 10/2008.
G829 XWS	Sold to Gwyn Williams Coaches (183), Lower Tumble, Carmarthenshire, 7/2009.
Y586 TOV	Re-registered V2 FOS - 11/2008.
V2 FOS	Re-registered Y586 TOV - 10/2013, in preparation for its sale.
Y586 TOV	Sold to Cavern City. Liverpool, 12/2013.
PUI 3785	Sold to Taylor. Yeovil, Somerset, 7/2010.
M734 BSJ	Sold to M. Hayward. Carmarthen, for scrap, 12/2009.
BX56 XAL	Re-registered DS56 FOS before entering service, 4/2009.
DS56 FOS	Re-registered BX56 XAL upon sale, 8/2015.
BX56 XAL	Sold to Morris Travel. Carmarthen as BX56 XAL in 8/2015.
R705 MNU	Not operated. Sold to F.E. Lewis, Whitland, 8/2009. To T.S. Lewis, Rhydlewis, Ceredigion, 11/2011.
WD03WVW	Re-registered B6 PRE - 9/2010.
B6 PRE	Re-registered WD03 WVW prior to sale, 7/2017.
WD03WVW	Sold to Evans Coaches. Steynton, Milford Haven, Pembrokeshire, 8/2017.
YJ59 NMZ	Sold to D. Jones. Acrefair, Wrexham, Clwyd, 7/2013.
VU03 ZPS	Returned to 'Next Bus'. Chippenham, Wilts, off hire, 3/2010.
YJ59 NNY	Sold to Gwynfor Coaches. Gaerwen, Anglesey, 1/2019, and re-registered GSV 494. To YJ59 NNY in 2/20.
P501 RYM	Sold to Richards Bros. Cardigan. 2/2011.
EJ52 UYS	Re-registered DSU 772 - 9/2010.
DSU 772	Re-registered EJ52 UYS - 12/2017, in preparation for sale.
EJ52 UYS	Sold to Lixnaw Coaches. Co Kerry, Irish Republic, 3/2018, re-registered 02-KY-10223.
N711 AHP	Sold to A & B Coach Travel, Ely, Cardiff, 10/2014. To Creigiau Travel, Creigiau, Cardiff, 9/2018.
DS11 FOS	Current
X847 XDE	Sold to 'Talley Ho' Coaches. Kingsbridge, Devon, 8/2016.
X848 XDE	Sold to 'Talley Ho' Coaches. Kingsbridge, Devon, 8/2016.
YJ06 YSG	Returned to Optare (dealer), Sherburn-in-Elmet, ex loan - 11/2011.
P564 PNE	Sold to M. Hayward. Carmarthen for scrap, 10/2012. To Davies Coaches. Llanelli, for spares 10/2012. Remains scrapped 6/2018. (See photograph on next page).
MP51 BUZ	Sold to Morris Travel. Carmarthen, with service 227, in 10/2013.
SF55 PSY	Sold to Bysiau Cwm-Taf, Whitland, 8/2019.
YJ08 ECX	Re-registered FF05 BUS – 10/2013.
FF05 BUS	Re-registered YJ08 ECX – 1/2016, in preparation for sale.
YJ08 ECX	Sold to Bennett's. Stafford. 2/2016.
FN09 AOA	Re-registered V2 FOS – 7/2014.
V2 FOS	Current
YJ55 YGX	Sold to Lawson. Corby, Northants, 12/2018.
M326 KRY XUD 367	Re-acquired from Davies Coaches, Llanelli, still carrying cherished registration plates JIL7657, but the transfer to its original identity, M326 KRY, had already taken place. Re-registered XUD 367 – 8/2016. Sold with the cherished registration to Evans. Steynton, Milford Haven, in 4/2018. However, the registration mark XUD 367 was re-purchased from Hayward, Carmarthen, in 2020, after the coach passed to him in 4/2019.

Above: This 1997 Mercedes-Benz 'Vario' 0814D, **P564 PNE**, operated for 6 months at Ffoshelig Coaches, before it was sold to Hayward, Carmarthen, for scrap in 10/2012, but passed to Davies Coaches, Llanelli, as seen, for spares. *(V. Morgan)*

YV07 PVJ **DS56 FOS** **YV07 PVJ**	Re-registered **DS56 FOS** - 9/2015. Re-registered **YV07 PVJ** upon sale - 3/2020. Sold to Bysiau Cwm-Taf, Whitland, as **YV07 PVJ**, 3/2020, and re-registered by them to **BC06 TAF**, before entering service in 3/2020.
RE65 FOS	Current
BL16 FYV	Returned to Evobus (dealer), Coventry, ex loan - 8/2016.
OU16 EWW	Returned to MAN (dealer), Trafford Park, Greater Manchester, ex loan - 9/2016.
BV55 FPN **FF05 BUS**	Re-registered **FF05 BUS** - 9/2016. Current
YN54 DDV	Sold to R. Spiller (2 Impress Travel), St Clears, Carmarthenshire, 8/2018.
WA11 HXL **B6 PRE**	Re-registered **B6 PRE** - 12/2017. Current
YN58 CFX **B10 PRE**	Re-registered **B10 PRE** - 9/2018. Current
YN60 FMG **DSU 772**	Re-registered **DSU 772** - 11/2018. Current
BF67 WLK	Returned to Evobus (dealer), Coventry, ex loan - 1/2019.
YN59 BMO	Current
K51 TER	Current
MIG 1727	Sold to M. Hayward (dealer), Carmarthen, 10/2020, in exchange for Setra, **BU51 FXF**.
SN53 ETR	Returned to Morris Travel, Carmarthen, ex loan - 10/2019. Sold to Ammanford Metals for scrap, 10/2019.
KP51 SXV	Returned to Morris Travel, Carmarthen, ex loan - 10/2019. Sold to Ammanford Metals for scrap, 10/2019.
BU51 FXF **XUD 367**	Re-registered **XUD 367** – 11/2020. Current
NDE 916R	Currently undergoing restoration.

Above: As this publication was nearing completion in April 2021, Rhodri Evans acquired this ECW bodied Bristol LH6L, registered **NDE 916R**, for preservation. It had been new to Daniel Jones & Sons, of Abergwili Road Garage, Carmarthen, in February 1977, passing to Davies Bros, Pencader, in April 1978, with the Daniel Jones business. See below.

Above: **NDE 916R** (121) received 3 different styles of Davies Bros livery, and all-over advertising livery, during its 17 years with Davies Bros. This style being the ultimate one before departure from Carmarthen, for pastures new at Worksop, and finally a driver trainer at Cheadle. I had the privilage of being the last Davies Bros employee to use it in passenger service, July 1995, on the Carmarthen - Llanelli 131 route. It will be interesting to see which livery it will receive.

VEHICLE PHOTOGRAPH INDEX

Reg. No.	Page No.	Reg. No.	Page No.	Reg. No.	Page No.	Reg. No.	Page No.
ARR 956Y	84	E345 EVH	68	MIG 1727	147/148	TH 2283	16
ASB 658	31	FDE 623	25	MP51 BUZ	133	TH 2510	14
ATU 56F	48	FFP 200V	50	MPG 153P	73	TIL 4527	96
A10 SBK	95/96	FF05 BUS	105	MUH 140	38	TNP 6V	61/62
A233 GNR	68	FF05 BUS *	134	MUI 7389	99	TTH 57	38
A475 TBX	103	FF05 BUS *	140	MX53 ZWD	109	TX 8740	14
BEX 350	34	GDE 416W	88	MX04 VLT	112	UKG 423S	72
BF67 WLK	145	GMS 305S	77	M326 KRY	136	VCH 165	43
BL16 FYV	139	G829 XWS	115	M734 BSJ	117	VFH 700S	60
BTH 777	19	HB 7491	35	M794 MTH	77	VIL 9911	110
BU51 FXF	150	HB 7518	35	NBX 581	47	VJU 259X	53/61
BU56 OOD	111	HCJ 273	28	NBX 666R	53	V2 FOS	92
BX 7410	10/11/12	HSG 231	28	NDE 916R	174	V2 FOS *	116
B6 PRE	123	HIL 2329	98	NDW 147X	85	V2 FOS *	135
B6 PRE *	143/151	HVJ 146N	44	NFR 837	47	V35 LDE	92
B10 PRE	144	IIL 8521	99	N50 PDE	110	WD03 WVW	122
B665 OFP	82	JDK 216	33	N711 AHP	128	WJB 490	88
CV02 LTA	101	JIL 2433	89	OBX 125J	52	WUX 658K	49
C826 CBU	74	JIL 7657	136	OJD 54R	67	XTH 700M	41/48/79/168
DBD 936	26	JLJ 109V	97	OKH 507	32	XUD 367	137
DBD 940	27	JRN 500	33	OKJ 958	37	XUD 367 *	150/151
DRH 122C	42	JTU 229T	93	OU16 EWW	141	XUY 59V	75/84
DS11 FOS	129	JUH 229W	85/86	PUI 3785	115	X847 XDE	132
DS56 FOS	121	JUI 1720	93/94	P501 RYM	125	X848 XDE	133
DS56 FOS	137/138	JUI 5931	109	P564 PNE	173	YCV 197	39
DSU 772	87	JUO 608	36	RAZ 9859	87	YIL 8181	112
DSU 772 *	90	KHN 730D	48	RE57 FOS	114	YJ55 YGX	135
DSU 772 *	97	KUI 1372	94	RE65 FOS	138/139	YJ07 EGD	114
DSU 772 *	127	KUY 442X	63/64/83	R6 RLC	104	YJ59 NMZ	124
DSU 772 *	144	KXI 318	98	R91 GWO	102	YJ59 NNY	125
DTH 999	22/29	K51 TER	146/147	R705 MNU	123	YMU 134	82
D422 JDB	64	LIL 9924	91	SCD 693X	108/152	YN53 VBO	107
EBX 666	22/23	LPU 620	25/26	SF55 PSY	134	YN54 DDV	142
EJ52 UYS	128	LTR 997R	61	STH 800K	40	YN59 BMO	146
EMB 151K	51	LUA 541	30	STT 413R	63/83/159	YSU 366	102/103
ETH 888	22/24	LUN 528F	42/43	SX 5044	20/22	125 WRR	37
EUJ 855	34	L975 VDE	105	TH 1068	15	608 CYS	49
E238 MBX	69	MBX 381P	45/46/169	TH 1928	15	6610 PT	39/40

*denotes a re-issued cherished registration number.